PRAISE FOR THE BOOK OF CEREMONIES

"The primal wisdom that emanates from these ancient teachings lifts up the spiritual practice of reverence — one that is often lacking in modern times. Horn demonstrates a kind of radical amazement, a deep feeling tinged with both awe and wonder as he sees the sacred in all things. These ceremonies touch the heart because they arise out of a felt sense of participation in the universe, a kinship with all beings and with matter."

— *Spirituality & Health*

"Horn's voice is graceful and elegant, and his concern for the natural world is predominant.... The essays and poems in this collection, which would make a good gift book, are meaningful, and the American Indian tone is meditative and enriching."

— *St. Petersburg Times*

"This is a beautiful and inspiring book in which Gabriel Horn shows us a way to become more spiritual through ceremonies based on Native American teachings from many different sources.... *The Book of Ceremonies* is a great read for anyone interested in the Native way of life...."

— *Chico News & Review*

THE BOOK OF CEREMONIES

By the Author

Native Heart
Contemplations of a Primal Mind

For Children:

The Great Change
Ceremony in the Circle of Life
The Native People/Native Ways Series:
    The Book of Knowledge
    The Book of Life
    The Book of Change
    The Book of Wisdom

THE BOOK OF CEREMONIES

A Native Way of Honoring and Living the Sacred

GABRIEL HORN

Art by
CARISES HORN

NEW WORLD LIBRARY
NOVATO, CALIFORNIA

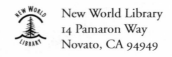

New World Library
14 Pamaron Way
Novato, CA 94949

Editor: Marc Allen
Cover design: Kathy Warinner
Text design: Mary Ann Casler

Library of Congress Cataloging-in-Publication Data
Horn, Gabriel, 1947–
The book of ceremonies : a native way of honoring and living the sacred / Gabriel Horn;
art by Carises Horn.
p. cm.
ISBN 978-1-57731-504-9
1. Indians of North America—Rites and Ceremonies. 2. Indians of North America—
Religion. 3. Indian philosophy—North America. I. Title.
E98.R3 H75 2000   00-055896
299'.74—dc21

First printing, August 2000

First paperback printing, May 2005

ISBN 978-1-57731-504-9

♻ Printed in Canada on 100% postconsumer waste recycled paper

▯ A proud member of the Green Press Initiative

10 9 8 7 6 5 4 3 2

TABLE OF CONTENTS

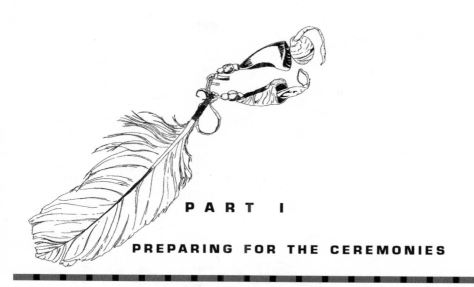

PART I

PREPARING FOR THE CEREMONIES

*For after all the great religions
have been revealed by brilliant scholars,
or have been written in books and embellished
in fine language with finer covers,
man — all mankind — is still confronted with
the Great Mystery.*

— Luther Standing Bear
Land of the Spotted Eagle

1

OUR UNLIMITED POTENTIAL

No hierarchy of life exists, no superior life forms,
just equal parts that make up the whole.

— Albert Einstein

We gaze up at the night sky, miles away from the artificial lights of the civilized world, and we cast our eyes toward the distant heavens and the realm of unimaginable space and unlimited possibilities. We stare up at the expanse of an infinite universe with countless stars suspended in the void, and we are connected to Time and Hope, like junctures of light in the deep dark ocean of space.

The great star we call our sun holds us in his influence as we float along on Mother Earth, spinning in cycles within this black celestial sea of nothingness. In all this we feel our own sense of place, surprisingly secure, cradled between her and the all-covering Father Sky. Our physical realities dwell here, limited and confined to these human forms, with the exception of that part of ourselves that draws sustenance from moments like this, when we gaze upon the heavens and suddenly become aware of the part of ourselves that connects us, as with the silken strands of a spider's web, to all things, great and small, and provides us the gift of potential we have within to expand and explore.

Infinity and eternity are abstractions beyond the intellectual limitations of humankind. In a universe wide as daylight, immense as darkness, there are no boundaries. There are no limitations. These come only when we attempt to define what we cannot. In a universe beyond our comprehension, the potential for our spiritual growth is restricted only by the physical forms we occupy and by the way we allow ourselves to think — but the Great Mystery, regardless, remains forever unending and eternal.

We share life simultaneously with all things in a Totality without beginning and without end — this is a humbling notion, but the humility we experience when we realize it helps us transcend into a greater sense of Place and Purpose, and into a sacred responsibility for being alive, and a part of it all.

In the beginning it flowed through the primordial
bloodstream of humankind. And long ago, whether
through ceremony or through simply gazing
at the night sky, the First People became
consciously aware of their place in the
Wheel of Life. They recognized their
connection to the vast subconscious,
and to various dimensions of Time and
Space and Spirit and Mystery, through the
power of their conscious awareness, and through the urgings of their
Original Instruction.

Long ago they sat together in a circle, passing sacred objects from
hand to hand, or they stood alone and turned their thoughts toward the
rising sun. They traced the natural movement of the sun across the sky,
setting into motion an harmonic flow or movement within the ceremonial circles they had formed, and within their own lives as well.

Long ago they knew the circle they created with others, and the
sunwise movement they imitated, and everything else in Ceremony
represents something, and draws special powers for specific purposes.

Long ago they became consciously aware that every song expresses
certain feelings, and entreats certain elements to come into the world.

Every prayer is a seed planted in the Mystery. Each one addresses some aspect of our needs and urgings, and prepares the world in a mysterious way, as if it were a garden, for its fulfillment.

Long ago they knew every color has a meaning; every feather, every bone, every beaded or quilled design has a unique power and significance.

They knew their instruments were special, each one made out of a desire to re-create the music of nature, each with a vibration and sound that was unique to itself and that drew attention to and from those troublesome or benevolent spirits and incorporeal beings that inhabited their world.

Long ago all of these elements of ceremony intertwined and became one with their intentions and purpose. Each one commanded their respect and appreciation. And so their seeds of prayer gestated, were born, and were made ready for fruition within the sacred awareness of Ceremony.

Times have changed, but certain elements of the human condition have not. No matter how civilized we humans have become, certain needs still flow through our primordial blood. And many are now seeking to satisfy their need for ceremony once again. But can we reconcile our sacred relationship to all things with the way we have chosen to live?

Anyone who chooses can learn to conduct aspects of ceremony. Anyone who chooses can purchase a Native American pipe. Anyone who chooses can buy a braid of sweetgrass, a bag of sage, or a stick of cedar. Anyone who chooses can gather feathers and collect fetishes. Anyone who chooses can learn to sing a traditional song, use a traditional instrument, or listen to traditional melodies of the flute on the latest digital disc. Anyone who chooses can learn words of prayer and supplication.

Chain bookstores display how-to books that teach anyone who chooses how to make things once handed down in more personal ways. They show you how to make "your own spirit mask." They show how to make a drum, how to make dream catchers. They sell kits to make your own flute.

Specially priced trips to temples and pyramids and other "power places" and "holy places" all over the world beckon from the Internet. Advertisements for guided and supervised "vision quest weekends" are scattered throughout the pages of New Age magazines.

To judge the right or wrong of all this or to criticize anyone does not serve the purpose and intention of this book. The heart knows what is true. These things may be good for some people and bad for others, right for some and wrong for others, but one thing cannot be denied: certain elements of ceremony cannot be sold or purchased. The most critical of all these are the elements that emanate from a good heart, from the intentions of the good-hearted people that have been brought into that Time and Space of Ceremony and share a belief in the interrelationship of all things.

And though anyone who chooses can purchase the conduits of ceremony, not everyone can enter into a ceremonial state of consciousness. To do this one must be of good heart, whether that heart is celebratory and joyous or anguished and sad. The purity of the heart and the sincerity of intentions are the master facts; they are essential. They are vital, as is a conscious awareness of one's relationship to all the things within the ceremony — for we enter into a ceremonial state of consciousness out of love and reverence for the sacredness and the beauty and the power of life and life's journey, no matter how grand or small that life may be, or how wonderful or difficult that road is to walk.

We enter into a ceremonial state of consciousness with respect for life, and for the purpose of well-being and balance, not only within our own lives, but for the Earth, our Mother, as well. A ceremony, even of one, then becomes an expression of gratitude and an acknowledgment of the sacred. It is a way of addressing and entreating the spirit of benevolence. It is a way of living.

Nearly every animated life form incorporates ritual of some kind. The ceremonial aspect of that ritual embodies that life form's conscious awareness and recognition of the sacred. The sacred emanates from a particular place and moment of mind that, for whatever reason, makes a conscious connection to the Great Mystery that all things share.

There is a remarkable scene in the book *Our Kinship with the Animals.* Gary Kowolski, a Unitarian minister and animal rights advocate, describes the observations of a zoologist who was caught early one evening by the splendor of an incredible sunset in an African rain forest. While he was appreciating the moment, he saw a lone chimpanzee come into the scene, cradling a papaya close to his body.

The chimp paused at an opening between the trees that provided an especially impressive view. "For a full fifteen minutes, the animal remained spellbound by the spectacle of the changing colors of the dusk and watched them without moving."

Then something wonderful happened, something that could help civilized humans become more aware of their own primal source and that of other life forms as well. The chimp, after his motionless observance of the setting sun, gently placed his papaya on the ground where he stood and left it there, heading back into the thicket, as silent as the evening breeze.

A ceremony? Perhaps. The significance of this and similar incidents among animals has been debated for ages among scientists and theologians. They argue whether or not these are truly occurrences in Time and Space when nonhuman life forms connect with conscious awareness to something sacred.

Some say that the magic of the moment affected the chimp so deeply that he wandered off, forgetting the papaya. Others say the chimp's reaction must have been completely unrelated to the sunset and that he simply lost interest in the papaya and left it on the ground where he had been standing.

But some of us feel that in some way the chimp left the papaya as an offering, a gift to the beauty of the place and to the Mystery of it all. Perhaps he even brought the treasured papaya there with that intention.

Perhaps he truly was honoring and expressing his gratitude for the sacred, and perhaps this is a primal element of our own nature, deeply rooted in our animal DNA. It does appear that the chimp, whether conscious of it or not, was doing something that our elders insist upon: We must never take from the world without expressing our gratitude, and without giving something back.

Maybe, as in the spring equinox story of "The Old Woman Who Was Young," the seed of this kind of acknowledgment is something that was nourished by the knowledge we acquired from our elder and wiser relatives, the animals, a very long time ago.

But maybe such a seed was simply planted by the Great Mystery in the beginning to provide us with our Original Instruction and Purpose within the Wheel of Life itself.

I don't believe humankind can ever completely surrender our ways of acknowledging and honoring this awareness. If we did, we would become so civilized that we would no longer live with a conscious reverence and respect for our relationship to the greater web of life outside ourselves. We would no longer allow the magic in the Mystery to stir our imaginations and creativity. We would no longer feel our connectedness to life, or our sense of wonder and appreciation for life. We would no longer be challenged to grow further as spiritual beings in these physical forms.

If we surrender our ways of acknowledging and honoring the sacred, then how would we come closer to the understandings and insights that enable us to grow? How would we be able to help ourselves heal and become whole after being hurt and broken?

And if we surrender our ways of acknowledging and honoring the sacred, then what would be the Purpose of our existence? What would be the Purpose for living?

Something sacred and mysterious connects us all, human and nonhuman, corporeal and incorporeal beings alike, and these moments of recognition occur among a great diversity of life forms in Time and Space, moments when that sacred union, that sense of ineffable Oneness, is pronounced and appreciated and realized.

It is natural in these moments to offer something in gratitude.

May *The Book of Ceremonies* be such an offering.

2

THE GREAT HOLY MYSTERY

Before the Beginning of the New Making, Awonawilona solely had being. Nothing else existed, save everywhere black darkness and everywhere void desolation. Then something happened. Awonawilona conceived within the Mystery of its own being and thought outward into space, and it was a New Beginning.

He stood on the beach, barefoot in the sand, and faced the rising sun, whose first rays were appearing from behind the dunes. It was not every morning that he was here at dawn, but today he felt the need. For too many things of the civilized world seemed to conspire against his natural being. Too many demands. Too much frustration. He needed to be here now. He needed to remind himself of what is truly important in life, and to reconnect to these things and to what is beautiful.

He needed to make a ceremony.

To honor the life that we live...

He says this to himself, as though responding to a question some-one has asked. He stands on the wondrous shore where Time, like the sea, is ever constant and forever changing, where the windswept sands cover the mind's traces of what was, what is, and what might be, and he turns toward the water that is always.

He turns in the direction of the Morning Star, and of the diverse realities and possibilities of this human experience, where the Sky and the Sea meet at the horizon and become one within an endless circle of wholeness, perfectly balanced, perfectly complete. He cries out, aloud this time,

"Thank you for this life I've lived! Thank you for the abundance of goodness that will surely come."

The acknowledgment springs from a deep place within, a sacred place where the conscious merges with the subconscious — the place where ceremony emanates. And then he says it again, with his arms raised, staring up at the sky, his outstretched hands opened,

"Thank you!"

He is addressing the universe, calling out to the Great Mystery that is the life and spirit within all things he has ever known and all things that, as a man, he can never know.

Like the seagulls who serenade the day above him, like the morning wind that rattles the fronds of the sabal palms behind him, like the Morning Star that rises to greet the dawn in the distance before him, he too acknowledges the beauty and blessings of this life, even now as he struggles again to understand his place in it all.

As the warmth of the sun embraces him and the summer breeze lifts the strands of his hair, a feeling of gratitude for life overwhelms him. And though he feels burdened with all that he has loved and lost, with all the struggles he has endured and the battles he has fought, he faces the horizon of Sky and Sea, and cries out once more,

"Thank you! Thank you for the blessings and sustenance that you have given. Thank you for the abundance of goodness that will surely come."

The first prayer simply expresses gratitude for all that has enabled him to live and for all those who have loved him. These last words express his faith that he will continue to be taken care of on the Path of Beauty, that the Earth will endure, and that he is not to worry — for that would create a sense of fear, and that kind of fear, he was taught, will block the abundance of goodness that is always there in the Mystery.

Something in the words, the sea, the morning sun allows him to surrender, once again, to the natural flow of the Mystery and to let go of the illusion of control and to know that, within this cosmic Totality that always was and will always be, there is always balance in the Oneness of All Things.

With this awareness, the words he first said to himself — *To honor the life that we live* — become suddenly whole within his being. The simple sentence fragment becomes an understanding of completeness.

And yet it is even more than this. It is more than acknowledging the beauty and the need for balance within all life, including his own — it is a sense of knowing that the decisions that have determined the path of his life have been based on a primal awareness that connects him in a mysterious and magical way to all things.

Within this awareness, he understands that as long as his decisions are based on giving and sharing, based on a partnership with all of life, he will never lose his way. He had learned long ago about the hypocrisy of those who take and use the idea of ceremony, yet live separated from its intent.

He had experienced the arrogance and greed of men and women whose past has diminished their spirit, and he, like all other forms of natural life, had suffered from the destructive nature of such people. That is why this ceremony at the light of dawn is needed, for ceremony helps to heal him, and reminds him that he can still walk the Path of Beauty.

Ceremony helps protect him too from those who have, through their lack of understanding, intellectually severed their ties with the natural world. It helps protect him from those who are driven by fears of scarcity, or hemmed in by feelings of superiority, or led into denial, or fragmented and frustrated within their own identities. Ceremony connects him now in a conscious awareness of All That Is Beautiful. Ceremony helps to keep him whole, so he can help bring balance to this world again.

It has always hurt him to think about the pain inflicted on this earth by men and women who have deprived themselves of spirit, and who have sacrificed their souls to the material world and the culture of consumption.

To honor the life that we live.

The fragment falls like a down feather through the space of his mind. And then he says again,

"Thank you for this life, and for the abundance of goodness that will surely come."

It is his incantation, of sorts, and he believes with all his heart and soul that in this way he is helping to re-create a balance, not only within himself, but within the world as well. This is the balance he seeks, the balance that acknowledges the sacred, like the holy power of the mighty Sun, and how it is able to heal even Chernobyl's radiation as it bleeds into the land and waters of the Earth. He believes that words of respect and recognition of life can still help to bring back the balance, that as long as the Earth and the forces that protect her can still feel and hear the vibrations of love coming from her people, the balance will come back.

He does not doubt this, for he has been taught by the elders that words have power, that the sounds of his words at this moment as he stands on this shore, and the intent that carries the words into the Mystery, are much more than feathery fragments or simple statements of prayer from a dying way of life. The ceremony of these simple words is a way of being. When we honor the sacred, we maintain the balance in our lives.

Like the first sound that gave origin to the New Beginning, the word manifested out of the Mystery into a symphony of cosmic mist that would form a universe without beginning and without end.

And so he cries out for the last time as he stands before the Sky, the Sea, the Earth, and the Sun,

"Thank you! Thank you for this life I have lived and for the abundance of goodness that will surely come."

SENSING
THE GREAT HOLY MYSTERY

TOUCH

The tug of a child's hands at your feet, the caress of your lover, the lick of your dog's tongue on your cheek, the feel of your cat's fur through your fingers, the embrace of a friend...

The joy when we're happy, the anguish in our hearts when they've been broken, the tears from our eyes, the fear we've known, the bones beneath the skin of those who are starving, a mother's pain during childbirth...

All that we touch, all that we feel, is evidence of its existence. For Wah'kon-tah exists in all things and all things exist within Wah'kon-tah.

SIGHT

The slant of the autumn sun, the sky through the window of a jet, the sunrise on the Great Plains, the sunset in the ocean...

The full moon on a clear night just above the horizon, a rainbow after a summer storm, the flicker of a firefly...

The darkness that precedes a hurricane, the despair in the faces of the needy, the raging flames of a burning forest, the black toxic smoke swirling toward the sky from the oil fields of Kuwait...

All that we see, all that we have seen, is evidence of its existence. For Wah'kon-tah exists in all things and all things exist within Wah'kon-tah.

SMELL

A sea breeze in the summer, the aroma of rich coffee brewing on a cold morning, the fragrance of roses, the smells radiating from your kitchen on Thanksgiving Day...

The sweet scent of pines in a forest, the pungency of a bay at low tide, the putridness of the corpses along the roadsides of Mozambique, the odor of cigarette smoke, the stink from the residue of paper mills, the stench of sewage treatment, the heavy traces of exhaust fumes...

All that we smell is evidence of its existence. For Wah'kon-tah exists in all things and all things exist within Wah'kon-tah.

TASTE

Chocolate syrup dripping down a heap of vanilla ice cream, yellow corn shining with butter, the juice of the strawberry, green beans, squash, a sweet potato, maple syrup...

The sting of lime, the bite of lemon, crab apples, bitterroot tea when you are sick, the heat of whiskey, the bite of betrayal, anger that burns your stomach...

All that we taste is evidence of its existence. For Wah'kon-tah exists in all things and all things exist within Wah'kon-tah.

SOUND

Thunder in a storm, the crack of lightning, the burst of a dolphin's breath, the swish of waves on the shore, the quiet of a mountain lake, a loon's haunting call, an eagle's fierce cry, the hiss of water on the rocks in the lodge of purification...

A mockingbird's song in spring, the laughter of children, the melody of a flute, the beating of a drum, the words of our prayers...

The cries of those in pain, the scream of chain saws, the whining diesels at the edge of the Everglades, the shattering sounds of helicopter gunships strafing villages in the Amazon or shaking homes of Northern Ireland at dawn, the blast of a land mine in a backyard in Bosnia, the explosions of atomic bombs, the pop of a handgun down the street where you live...

The slap of a hand, the roar of the wind at its greatest strength, the rumble of the quaking earth, the silence between the stars...

All that we hear is evidence of its existence. For Wah'kon-tah exists in all things and all things exist within Wah'kon-tah.

It is the Great Holy Mystery, the sum total of all things, the collective Totality that always was, without beginning, without end.

It is the inexplicable sharing-togetherness that makes all things, animate and inanimate, of equal value, equal importance, and equal consequence, because everything is Wah'kon-tah simultaneously, and collectively creates the form of the Great Holy Mystery, unimaginable and incomprehensible, forever and unending.

3

A ZUÑI CREATION ACCOUNT

*The Genesis of the Worlds,
or the Beginning of Newness,
according to the Zuñi*

Before the beginning of the new-making, Awonawilona, the Maker and Container of All, solely had being. There was nothing else whatsoever throughout the great space of the eternal ages save everywhere black darkness, and everywhere void desolation.

In the beginning of the new-made, Awonawilona conceived within its own being and thought outward into space, whereby mists of increase, steams potent with growth, were evolved and uplifted.

Thus, by means of innate knowledge, the All-Container made

itself in the person and form of the Sun, whom we hold to be our father and who thus came to exist and appear.

With his appearance came the brightening of the spaces with light, and with the brightening of the spaces the great mist-clouds were thickened together and fell, whereby was evolved water in water — yea, and the world holding sea.

With his substance of flesh outdrawn from the surface of his person, the Sun-Father formed the seed-stuff of twain worlds, impregnating therewith the great waters — and lo! — in the heat of his light these waters of the sea grew green and scums rose upon them, waxing wide and weighty until — behold! — they became Awiltelin Tsita, the Four-Fold Containing Mother Earth, and Apoyan Tachu, the All-Covering Father Sky.

4

THE CIRCLE

Without Beginning, Without End

No man or woman aware of the Great Mystery can fully conceive of it; no one could ever draw its picture. After all, who can imagine the Origin of the Universe, the First Cause of All, the Infinite that always was and always will be? And who can imagine what the sum total of all things in the universe living simultaneously together looks like? It is far beyond what is humanly conceivable.

Yet, we are going through an evolutionary process of understanding, and wisdom has unfolded and revealed its beauty, like the bud of a rose on a warm summer day. We find great meaning in symbols, and the Circle has become the closest representation of the Mystery of Mysteries, for its sacred form symbolizes oneness, wholeness, and totality. It is the path that is without beginning and without end. It is eternal. It encompasses all things: beginnings and movement, closure and completeness, fulfillment and fruition. It is the struggling of the seed, it is the promise within the bud, it is the beauty of the bloom.

When we become part of a Circle, a sense of connectedness and awareness is created. Experience and memory, present and past, intertwine. It reveals a kind of wisdom, one that results from observation.

For the Moon is round; the Earth is round. The Moon travels around the Earth in a circle. The Earth rotates around the mighty Sun, which is also round. And all the planets of the Sun travel in circles, with their moons and rings in circles around them.

And the billions of other suns, the stars we see scattered across the night sky, are all round and all are part of the great spiral of stars that create the form of the Milky Way, and the galaxy that is the Milky Way is a great spiral spinning in circles in a vast space strewn with countless more galaxies of countless stars and planets, all revolving in circles within circles within circles.

Stones, seashells, the trunks of trees, the path of the clouds, a drop of water, the arc of the rainbow; the single cell, the embryo of human life; the band of love around your mate's finger;

The sky-path of the Sun;

The beehive, the ant mound, an eagle's nest, the nest of the robin, the eggs of their unborn; the wind at its greatest power — circles within circles.

A holy man said, *Nature wants things to be round.*

The cycle of the seasons, the stages of life, the movement of the feathered dancers around the drum, which is round; the opening of the bowl of the pipe on which we pray; the lodge of our purification; the stones;

The forms of our ceremonies.

PART II

GREETING THE DAY,
ACKNOWLEDGMENT AND GRATITUDE

They reckon ill who leave me out:
When me they fly, I am the wings
I am the doubter and the doubt,
And I am the hymn, the Brahmin sings. . . .

— Ralph Waldo Emerson,
"Brahma"

5

THE PIPE AND THE TOBACCO

When the first people walked the earth, they were beginners in everything, and did not know very much. Okabewis (the Messenger, in Ojibwa) was sent to them. Okabewis instructed them how to live. He brought the First People many gifts. Among them was the gift of tobacco and, most importantly, how it was to be used.

He cradles the deerskin bundle that embraces the stem in his arms as one would an infant. He holds the beaded bag that the bowl occupies in one hand, as though nothing could separate the bag from his grasp except his own will. All are precious objects. All are sacred. All is Manitou.

His eyes focus on the horizon and the first light of day. An early morning breeze feels like a caress from the dawn as he squats down near the ground and places the bundle and the bag in front of him upon the flesh of the Earth.

Slowly, the way the wind might unveil the moon from a blanket of clouds, he removes the bowl from its colorfully beaded protection.

Gently, the way a man might stroke the hair of his loved one, he unwraps the stem from its smooth covering and arranges the four eagle feathers fastened with sinew to the stem. Each feather serves as an intercessor to the Mystery, an evocation of power, a carrier of prayer.

A tiny bundle of calico is also fastened to the stem. It contains seeds and kernels from Mother Corn, Manomin (wild rice), sweet-grass, and cedar. These are the gifts from the nations of plants — nourishment and healing, purification and dreaming.

He touches the stem once again, and his consciousness shifts to the trees, and a sense of humility overcomes him. And he weeps within for his own deep appreciation of the sacrifices of all that have given life in order that people may live.

It is at times like this when ceremony reconnects us once again with the forgotten ways we need to be, and emotions of gratitude arise within like the billowy clouds of summer storms.

His tears drop a brief, reluctant rain, falling upon strands of wampum shells tied to the stem. How appropriate, he thinks, that his tears fall upon seashells, another circle within the great Circle of Life.

The smoothly cut purple shells symbolize sincerity in the thoughts we have at these times and in the words we speak, and they draw to him at this moment the spirit of the sea: the power of the waves, the gracefulness of the manta, the playful breath of the dolphin.

Many items decorate the stem, which spans the length of a child's arm. The tail of a white-tail deer hangs from it, and is the last thing he touches before he stands. His hands savor its texture, and it brings to mind the sacrifices of the animals, how they have served as the providers and teachers of the people.

He stands now in the light morning wind and holds up each object, bowl and stem, to the sky. Then, like the sea foam of a wave touching the shore, like the hands of two people joining in love, like a teardrop falling onto a seashell, he connects the stem and bowl together. He holds the pipe. It has become a living being.

On the ground near him is a small pouch, and he rests the pipe alongside it. He dips into the tiny bundle with his fingers and lifts out a pinch of tobacco. As he places this sacred herb in the bowl, he contemplates its sacrifice. He contemplates the gift of this sacred plant that helps his prayers to transcend into the Great Mystery, where they evolve in their own way into the physical.

All My Relations

Within my hand I hold my brother, father,
  grandfather, sister, mother, and grandmother.
Within my hand I hold the true spirit of giving.
Within my hand I hold knowledge of past and future.
Within my hand I hold the selflessness of sacrifice.
Within my hand I hold the hopes and prayers of life.
Within my hand I hold all my relations.
Within my hand is Tobacco.

— *Mark Self*

6

A MORNING PRAYER

To the East

> *In my mind, and with my body, I face your Direction,*
> *the place of the Daybreak Star.*
> *I hold the pipe of your breath, and raise it to you,*
> *with the bowl close to my heart.*
> *I am aware of the gifts of light and life*
> *that you provide each day of my life.*
> *I am conscious that today will be like no other,*
> *and I will acquire new experiences,*
> *each one allowing that part of me that is all things*
> *a chance to grow.*
> *As I place the stem of this living pipe to my lips*

I draw in my breath and breathe out my prayer
of awareness and gratitude.
For I stand before you whose Direction is the rising Sun,
whose season is the Spring,
and watch the smoke of my prayers
becoming one with your Power.
This day I am living in your Beauty.

TO THE SOUTH

In my mind, I follow the path of the Sun,
and I stand with the stem pointing now
in your Direction.
With the bowl close to me, I feel your Power coursing
through the warm streams of my lifeblood,
drumming strongly and peacefully
in my heart.
I am aware and conscious
of the warm wind caressing my skin
and of the seeds of promise and life
being carried in your essence.
As I place the stem to my lips

I breathe in your Power
and release my breath in the sacred smoke
of this living pipe with words that express
my gratitude to you,
whose Power is the vitality of life,
whose season is Summer,
for this day I am living in your Beauty.

TO THE WEST

In my mind,
I continue to travel the Sun's path,
and I stand tall facing your Direction,
conscious and aware that your Power
allows me to sleep and brings me the dreams
that guide my life with your Wisdom.
With the stem of this living pipe directed
at the brightest star in your Sky,
I am reminded of the hope you provide
in the darkness of my own fear.
I am reminded of my relationship
and connectedness with the universe;

though I am smaller than a grain of sand
on all the beaches of the earth,
I am part of it all.
As I place the stem of this pipe to my lips
and draw in your breath,
I release a wisp of smoke
that has become my thought in physical form.
I watch the smoke become my prayer of gratitude
to you, whose Power is maturity,
whose season is Autumn,
for this day I am living in your Beauty.

To the North

I complete the circle I have traveled in my mind,
and I stand now facing you,
whose Power washes over me
in cold cleansing waves of wind.
With the stem of this living pipe
I gesture in your Direction,
aware and fully conscious of the wisdom
that I have gathered in your presence,

wisdom my time on earth has granted me.
You teach me that there is no end to life,
but rather a transition and transcending
from this existence within an eternal circle
without beginning, without end.
With the bowl extended toward you,
away from me, I take a breath of smoke
and release my prayer of gratitude to you
for the time I have had in this life,
and for the struggles that have helped that part of me
that is all things to become stronger.
In this way I can help the future generations
to continue.
Please know that on this morning I am one with you,
whose Power is wisdom and Great Change,
whose season is Winter.

I express my thankfulness
for the life I live in your Beauty.

7

THE PATH OF BEAUTY

When we walk on the Path of Beauty, beauty comes from within us, for to walk this path is to understand and acknowledge the essence of beauty in all other forms of life as well.

We know it is not the nature of light to vanquish all darkness, nor the nature of good to conquer all evil, nor the nature of any species or beings to have dominion over any others. It is the nature of all things in the Mystery to find their place in the balance. This is the path of Beauty's Way.

Some have said that we have experienced all this before, that this is not the first time we have journeyed this earth walk. Perhaps this is true, perhaps we have done all this before, and we have a sense of it all happening again. Still, everything — past and present, tangible and illusory — happens now, for Time is of the Mystery, and all is really One.

To walk the path of Beauty's Way, we must remember to make ourselves aware of this present moment, to be attentive, to be grateful. For as we make this journey that is life, as we experience and appreciate the here and now, we walk the Path of Beauty.

8

SHE GREETS THE DAWN

Just before daybreak, she watches the pale slip of the waning moon rise above the dogwood and palms across the street. Hanwi is too slender to give much light, she thinks.

Shadows slip across the moon's face. Are they clouds or phantasms? She contemplates both, remaining still, watching while the sky lightens.

Above her, two doves perch on a telephone wire. She hears them murmuring, and reflects on her marriage, and on the man she sleeps with, and on Destiny unfolding.

Though the Sun has yet to show himself in person and form, his light tinges the undersides of the clouds a glowing ashen peach. She feels herself call out to him. Wake up, Grandfather!

For tonight Hanwi will hide her face and ready herself for another cycle, another circle of fullness.

Like the Moon when she caught the Sun making love to the Wind, once she too felt betrayed by her lover and wanted to hide her face in shame. But on this day, the Moon and she are beautiful together.

She knows this. She feels it. She has a sense of it.

And she's glad that she came out to greet the daybreak star — and instead was surprised by the Moon.

The cardinals take up the call now. Wake up! Wake up!

A mantle of clouds drifts along, concealing the slight crescent of Hanwi, and the horizon shows a sliver of fire.

Morning has arrived!

Even the crows are awake; their hard caws come from all directions in the neighborhood, and a mockingbird sings her entire repertoire.

The air tastes sweet, she thinks, and then she voices her first sounds since she opened her eyes from sleep.

"It is a good day," she whispers. "It is a good day to be alive."

9

THANKSGIVING RITUAL

Let us become aware of the beauty in our lives,
of the gifts we have been given,
of the time we have had together.
If we reflect on our struggles
and how they enabled us to grow,
if we close our eyes and see the blessings
of this world and this life,
if we feel a sense of gratitude,
we become aware of the beauty.

Whenever a ceremony begins, when the hearts of the people join in solemn and sacred prayer, or a council convenes to deliberate and decide on issues of the people, all those who assemble begin by expressing gratitude.

The etiquette of such occasions when individuals gather together involves a formal acknowledgment of the presence of all who have come, and a moment to remember our ancestors and relatives who have departed this existence in physical form but who remain with us in memory and in the spirit of All That Is.

An opening ritual echoes the collective voice of generations when we express our heartfelt gratitude to the Earth, our Mother, who sustains us and gives us the home where we dwell and experience the journey of our lives.

We acknowledge this wonderful gift of love by saying,

Thank you!

> *To the oceans and bays, to the currents and streams,*
> *to the quiet pools and lakes,*
> *To the fish, big and small,*
> *who have given of themselves that others may live,*
> *To the whales, our cetacean relatives,*
> *for their wisdom and the lessons of family*
> *they have taught us, for the gift of life they have given us,*

and to their cousins and our relatives, the dolphins,
for the joy they have brought us,
and the sense of Purpose they have shown us.
    To the Corn Mother and the yellow maize,
to the fruits and the berries,
to the medicinal plants and trees,
to the forests and the Standing Nations
for the shelter they provide and the air we breathe.
    To the animals, great and small,
who have served for food
and given unselfishly of themselves
that we may live, and who have shared
with us their power and their wisdom.
    To the birds, great and small,
whose feathers adorn us
and serve as intercessors of our prayers,
lifting our words to the heavens,
to the eagle whose bold flight inspires.
    To the tiny insects who help keep the balance,
    To our Father, the Sky,
who protects us and our Mother Earth,

To our elder relative, the mighty Sun,
who sustains us with light and warmth,
To the sacred Moon,
who influences the movement of the waters,
and the cycles of women and men and harvest.
To the great winds that sweep away
the illusions of our world
and of our self-importance,
and to the gentle breezes that caress our senses.
To the Thunder Beings,
To our relatives and messengers
who dwell among the Stars,
And to the Great Holy Mystery
who exists within all things
and is the life in all things,
whose abundance provides all that is useful
and who is forever the source and ruler
of health and life . . .

Thank you!

10

A CEREMONY OF OBSERVATION

"*Ho Whoah!*" she says, suddenly realizing that she doesn't know what day it is, and isn't even sure what month it is.

Pay attention to the solar and lunar timing, her grandmother had once told her. And she recalled watching the eclipse of the moon last month. It was awe-inspiring, unreal almost, for her to know that Grandmother Moon was there, though she was hidden in shadow, and she was unable to see her shining, wonderful face.

She had even felt an irrational fear, human and primal: *What if she is really gone? What if Grandmother doesn't return, if something unimaginable happens, and the moon disappears forever?* It had made her glad beyond words, thrilled, when she saw beautiful Hanwi again later that night, sailing the clouds.

She bends down and picks up one of the children's toys, a little plastic man. She puts it in her dress pocket while her thoughts drift back to the night before, when the Moon was fat and half full. How beautiful she was.

She remembered coming back into the house after going out to see her. She remembered how her husband silently greeted her from behind as she stood over the kitchen sink washing potatoes, how he lifted her hair and tenderly placed a silky strand behind her ear, and how, as the warm water ran over her hands, he kissed her neck.

She remembered how he held her, and how she felt herself fall into him, as he fell into her. It was a wonderful moment, she thought, closing her eyes. It might have lasted an eternity, and maybe it was just an instant. It was one of those moments when the timing was right.

She stands on the patio and looks out at the last streaks of sunset. She doesn't know what time it is, she isn't even quite sure of the month, only that it is almost summer, and that in a little while the moon will be full again. It will be the Strawberry Moon.

I just don't know, she says to herself. I just do not respond to linear time as a basic concept of existence. . . . I am on Indian time of the soul, I think.

She stands in the midst of piles of family laundry, but she looks around at the world. She sees the slanted rays of the sun as they reach through the mango trees in front of her. In the beams of golden sunset light, she sees two little squirrels tentatively exploring the ground.

These are my mother's children, she thinks to herself. *They are cared for by the trees, but they belong to the Earth.* She senses they have just fallen from their birth nest, and she calls out, "Be careful!"

They are so much like her children, she notices, hesitant, uncertain in new surroundings, yet courageous, even foolhardy. Now, like her children, they belong to the Earth too.

She greets the big crow who lands on a branch just above her head, and the blue jay that flits about. She can hear the woodpecker drumming not far away. She smiles as she remembers that they were all babies once, and they have survived long enough to get mates and raise new young.

"So it is never for nothing," she says aloud. It is her affirmation at the end of the day. A celebration for the continuation of life.

She reaches down and picks up a laundry basket and places it on the wood table next to her. The crow silently watches from his perch just above her. The squirrels suddenly pause. The woodpecker's drumming has ceased. The blue jay sways on a thin branch at the very top of the tree. Everything becomes still, and time rests.

She knows the long view is not easy to keep in mind, but she knows that the Mystery of Life provides a journey for us, where beginnings and ends of things move in perpetual motion in circles and cycles, and past, present, and future all intertwine, and transcend into one another, leading us inevitably to discover our greater sense of Purpose.

It's a rewarding path, she thinks to herself; it is full of itself, full within, full of encouragement, full of rewards for all those who pause to observe and to live on this kind of Indian time of the soul.

PART III

LOVE, MARRIAGE, AND DIVORCE

An Aztec Love Song

I know not whether thou hast been absent:
I lie down with thee, I rise up with thee,
In my dreams thou art with me.

If my eardrums tremble in my ear,
I know it is thee moving in my heart.

11

CEREMONY OF THE STORY

Magic Words

(Eskimo)

In the very earliest of times,
When both people and animals lived on the earth,
A person could become an animal if he wanted to
And an animal could become a human being.
Sometimes they were people
And sometimes animals
And there was no difference.
All spoke the same language.
That was the time when words were like magic.
The human mind had mysterious powers.
A word spoken by chance
Might have strange consequences.
It would suddenly come alive
And what people said wanted to happen could happen —
All you had to do was say it.
Nobody could explain this:
That's the way it was.

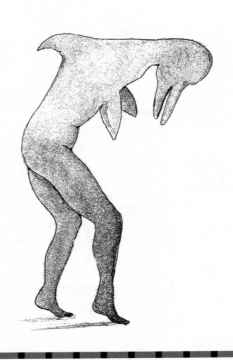

Once in a while a story needs to be told that can help change the world and make it new again. And in the retelling of such a story, there is ceremony. . . .

What is magic, if not the world?
What is the world, if not magic?

IT HAS BEEN SAID THAT...

From the edge of night she first saw him, tall and naked on the sand, newborn of the ocean, newborn of dawn. His gray skin glistened in the nacreous light, and his blowhole, covered in foam, engulfed the cool wind that circled and nested upon his head. She watched as he untangled the algae from his long raven hair, from his smooth belly and lithe sex, and she smiled as he timidly stepped his first steps. This was the most magnificent being the Moon had ever seen, and although time had come for her to make way for the Sun, a new feeling, more powerful than any other she had ever felt since the origin of her dance in the night Sky, left her poised on the horizon. She summoned all the strength that remained in her round, full form, and with a waning light she touched him, and turned the gray of his skin forever into a bright copper-brown.

He turned, his gaze holding her in suspense, just as she held the luminescent tide. The Moon knew then that she had been born to be two or none, and she longed for a mouth with which to kiss him, arms and legs with which to embrace him, breasts with which to nurse him, and a womb with which to shelter him, like the endless couples who nestled upon the Earth, comforted beneath the blanket of the Moon's silver light, night after night.

Finally, when the Sun became too fierce for the Moon to remain in the morning Sky, she faded away, with the image of the glorious man-dolphin wandering in the sand consuming her innermost being, and she fell asleep so that she could dream and thus be with the one she loved. And in her sleep, she dreamed that she awakened....

He searched the dunes with his new eyes, naked, confused, afraid. Nothing was as he had foreseen. Only the stars reminded him of that place which was not this place, and of that time which was not this time, when after emerging from the water he would see the lights of sacred village fires wavering deep in the forest, as the old ones had taught him through the Ceremony of the Story. They said that along the tree line he would find clothes, that he should dress while the Moon set under the star quilt of the night, and conceal the blowhole at the top of his head with a colorful turban of her corn silk hair. They told him not to be afraid of the drum of his heart, pounding as though it were the heart of all humanity, merged with the drums of the forest.

Yet now, on the night of the fall equinox, the only lights he sees along the coast do not flicker from sacred fires, but radiate a flat lifeless glow over a world without forests, where scant palm trees cower around inert monoliths of stone that violate the very body of the Mother. Even the stars from the sacred darkness of the Father have lost their splendor in his unimagined world of chaotic, alien vibrations, a world gone Koyannaskaatsii.* And the sounds he hears come not from the drums in the forest, but from the strikes of his own frightened heart emanating through the top of his vulnerable blowhole.

While he removes the algae from his body and takes his first unsteady steps upon the wet sand, a soft, familiar light touches him. Its caress changes the hue of his skin from gray to a luminous bronze. The man who was once a dolphin gazes into the heavens, and there he sees her, waning on the horizon, round, still radiant. Her warmth awakens a comforting stir at the pit of his stomach, a sensation that assures him all is indeed in accordance with the ritual that initiated his rebirth as man, the ritual of the need.

* *Out of balance.*

A silent prayer of gratitude issues from his lips.

A few miles away, in a small apartment by the bay, a young woman awakens to the sound of her pounding heart. She sits on the edge of her bed with eyes still closed, entranced by the echo of a dream in which she was the Moon who swam with a dolphin. Together they played in the ocean, she a silver light who illumined the deep dark waters, he a graceful dancer upon her glorious stage. And when they embraced, the only light left in the world was in the dolphin's eyes, wherein she saw reflected the human form that the Moon had chosen so as to love him fully. In his eyes, the young mystified woman had seen the image of her own self.

She lays back in bed, startled by the moist sheets beneath her, by the wetness of her own body. She stares absently at the ceiling, and as her eyes slowly adjust to the dark star-lit room she feels as though another consciousness inhabits her, blissfully exploring her body with her own hands, pausing in the warmest curves, repeating the same paths over and over; discovering by touch the places where the skin was strong and firm, and where it was soft and hidden from daylight; where, on the throat, the heartbeat pulsed, and beneath the taut breasts, the breath roared; where the nerves shivered as her hands approached her yielding center of sensation.

Ancient memories unfold before her eyes, carrying her to another place and another time....

She sees herself surrounded by other young women whose painted faces are moonflowers glowing around a central fire. Their dark eyes sparkle with promise, and reflect the beauty of the encompassing circle of men who beat upon their drums, shake their rattles, play their flutes, and call out his secret name into the moonless night, for the lover is ready, and love must be fulfilled.

They say that...

In the three months that followed, the Moon gradually disappeared from the night Sky, causing much havoc and confusion. With no one to guide them, the tides rebelled, swallowing coastlines or uncovering mile after mile of reef. Women missed their cycles, creating a great imbalance in the wheel of birth and death. Scientists and mystics alike turned mute, ashamed at their inability to explain the unprecedented catastrophe. Lovers had to find refuge in other, less romantic lights, and everywhere, people prepared for the end of existence as they knew it.

An enormous cloud of fear smothered the entire planet.

But in a small, remote pocket of the Earth, a shaman, after spending five days in the other world, remembered what others had long forgotten. The dolphin man is back, said the old one to his people. The Moon is in love, and we must help her find her lover.

And so, guided by his vision and by his love for the Mystery, the first people held ceremonies for their union, night after night. They sang songs that they thought had been washed away by time, and they danced dances they could barely recall, all to help the woman who was the Moon and the man who was a dolphin bring their love to fruition. And as they lit their sacred fires, and beat their sacred drums, the Ceremony of the Story began to unfold once again.

A man stands alone on the shore of the Gulf of Mexico, making his offering to the frightened sea that had until recently been his home. As the sun sets, he speaks silently, assuring the tide that its beloved mistress would soon be back, for the Mystery had just granted him a dream. He tells the waters how in his dream a young woman poured love into his heart, and from that love a spirit was conceived that would set all things back into the sacred way of the Mystery. In my dream, he says, the spirits of dolphins, the spirits of stars, and the spirits of the ancestors gathered in what seemed like a great celebration that focused on a beautiful infant, who swam through the crystal light of a sacred world. All the while she swam, a shaman's song filled the watery air with magic, and the hearts of everyone filled with joy, and the essence of love filled all things. . . .

At his bare feet, the waves murmur the beginning of the song of night. Elsewhere, the drums signal the start of the Ceremony.

Inside her small apartment, she who was once a young woman hears and recognizes a song. She had been hearing these same drums and these same voices since the start of Autumn; bit by bit they had awakened her, until tonight, when she finds herself fully awake.

In preparation for her lover, she combs her rich black hair, dons a necklace of precious coral, several bracelets of quetzal feathers, and a silver dress woven from the light of her eager heart.

Guided by the song, the Moon leaves in pursuit of her destiny.

She approaches the man while he looks out over the darkened sea. The silence is as deep and immense as the night beyond them. Even before he faces her, the Moon feels the power of his gaze unveiling the secrets of her innermost being. He turns, and all the light of the world is in his eyes. Inside them she sees the Pleiades, and the sacred fires of the old ones. As they fill with tears, she sees reflected the beautiful woman whom she has chosen in order to love him more fully.

The man who was once a dolphin feels his heart expanding as though it were the heart of all humanity. While he contemplates the woman before him, his blowhole opens wide beneath his many braids, and the drum in his chest blends with the drums of the Ceremony.

Words pour from their eyes.

That night of the winter solstice, on a beach too cold for even the bravest of souls, a naked man and woman rest upon the lap of their Mother, drunk with the intimate elixir of their love. All of life celebrates this blessed union, for out of its sensuous purity a magical infant has been conceived.

And as the three of them sleep, the full Moon returns to the night Sky and shines warmth upon their dreams and magic upon the hearts of all beings who share the potential to love.

And the shaman sings....

So it was, and so it is, and so it will forever be....

1 2

FATHER SKY/MOTHER EARTH

An Omaha Love Song

*As the day comes forth from the night
So I come forth to seek thee.
Lift thine eyes and behold him
Who comes with the day to thee.*

And the shaman sings....
    So it was, and so it is, and so it will forever be....
The young man followed his uncle up the winding rocky slopes to a precipice overlooking the earth. They had been climbing for a while, so it felt good to sit on the cool ground and rest near a clump of sage.

The sky was brilliantly clear and blue. Hardly a cloud anywhere, save off in the west above the distant mountains. When he looked at the clouds, the young man felt the gathering of uncertainties.

"A man is not superior to anything," the uncle said, as if there had been a conversation going, when there had been nothing but silence. "So don't go into your marriage ceremony tomorrow thinking that your wife is anything less than your equal."

He picked up a dried twig, and held it with both hands. "The spirit of a woman can be broken in a marriage if that spirit is not nourished, if she's not respected and shown that she is loved." And he snapped the twig in two.

He reminded his nephew of husbands who would not help their wives with the chores of maintaining a home, or take time to spend with their children, or with their wives.

He said he'd seen some men grow fat with ego expecting their wives to do all the housework. He'd heard men say, "Housework is a woman's responsibility." He'd seen men leave their wives alone until they had needs only their wives could fulfill.

These men have forgotten that there was a time when even to be allowed to brush the hair of their wives was an honor the women bestowed on their husbands, and that others could tell how loved a married woman was by the beauty of her hair. These men no longer braid the hair of their wives, nor decorate it with fine feathers or strips of pretty pelts.

The nephew shook his head. "No," he said, "I won't be a husband who lets his wife do all the work at home, Uncle, and I am honored to brush her hair.... I love her. But what about all the work that I have to do?"

The uncle listened to the wind and stared off at the dark clouds gathering far away. He spread his arms out wide and breathed deeply. It was as if the pure air filled him up, and everything appeared clear to him.

"The Great Mystery is not a man," he said, smiling as if it were obvious. "That's where the big problem lies." He laughed with the release of another breath. "We don't believe we were made in the image of the First Cause of All That Is."

The uncle stood and gazed out at the vast earth and sky before him, his thumbs hooking the pockets of his jeans. He was well aware of the consequences of this kind of patriarchal thinking. He'd seen in his own life the result of that thinking — on women, on other men, on the earth.

"Men who see the world like that are the ones who think what they do is more important than anything else, that somehow they got to be the pinnacle of Creation."

He breathed deeply once again and shook his head slowly, like a man disgusted at something he had seen, something he was seeing again in his mind's eye. "Men who think like that, Nephew, are the ones who decide what lives and what dies. Men like that choose what's good for them, and destroy what doesn't serve their purpose."

He continued breathing deep, and now directed his breath in a vertical circle inside himself, releasing each one slowly.

He turned and faced the young man beside him. "It's that kind of ego," he said, "that gets them and this whole world in trouble, because it allows a man to force his will on another, to dominate, to think of himself as superior."

He looked back at the earth and sky. "It's not our way," he said, his words trailing off. He squatted back down by the clump of wild sage. "It's just not our way."

The nephew went up to the edge of the precipice and looked down over the earth. They had never climbed this far together, he thought.

"Look at this land you stand upon," the uncle said, with an outstretched hand. "Look all about you!"

"It's beautiful, Uncle."

"And it is your Mother."

The young man turned and gazed down at his uncle, who glanced up at him and smiled again.

"Do you see the sky, Nephew?" He raised his arm, and the young man's eyes lifted upward.

"This is your Father. Do you see it all?"

The uncle kept breathing in the sage-scented air as if to make each breath a conscious act. As he did it, he could feel his mind expanding with each sweet breath.

They sat together again, and the uncle talked about the equality of all things in the Mystery, and told his nephew what he had been taught when he was young and about to marry — that the Great Mystery is not a manlike being, but rather the Mystery of mysteries. He told his nephew that Earth and Sky are manifestations of the Mystery, through their own mysterious sexual process. Earth and Sky are equal beings with different roles, one no more important than the other. Together they create a balance on which all life as we know it depends.

He slowly stood again, stretching his legs. The young man beside him reminded him in so many ways of himself, in his turbulent youth.

"Nephew," he said, "seek balance in your marriage. Help each other. Never demean her. If either one of you demeans the other, you lose that balance."

"I will never demean her," he promised. But there was something else he had to ask. "Isn't it her job, though, to raise the children and care for the home, and mine to work and make money for us to live?"

"She will be the mother of your children, yes, and she'll pour her love into them. But she will have desires too, and dreams. Yes, she will have dreams, and the need to create and to have a sense of purpose will remain the essence of her life."

The uncle bent down and reached for a small leaf of sage from the bush near him. He rubbed the leaf between his fingers and held it to his nose. The fragrance carried a sense of goodness and well-being to his mind.

"Help her to raise the children, and recognize her needs as best you can. Encourage her to dream, and to create, and share with her the journey of it all."

He looked up at his nephew. "And remember," he said, "it's still an honor for a man to brush his wife's hair."

He remembered his own wife's hair, vividly. Even now, years after her death, he could still feel himself stroking it and holding it like strands of black corn silk in his hands. His words affirmed once again the balance of his own marriage, one that had lasted for many decades. And his words planted the seed of honoring one's mate deeper into the heart and spirit of his nephew, where it would take root and sprout and grow.

They stood together, embraced by the great blue Sky, embraced by the fertile Earth. They stood and quietly contemplated all there was to learn and all there was to know about marriage, the miraculous gift of sharing one's life with another.

They stood and stared off in the direction of the west. The dark clouds over the distant mountains had vanished.

13

MARRIAGE: OLD WAYS AND NEW WAYS

Sharing
(Ojibwa)

Come,
let us
drink.

S he placed her basket of strawberries on the kitchen table, went into her bedroom for her little pipe, and headed outside to the backyard, where her granddaughter was seated alongside her future husband. The young woman and the young man sat upon old stones that formed an old circle around an ash pit where many fires had burned in ceremonies over time. They were awaiting the grand-mother's blessing, the elder's approval, often tacit and subtle, that helps so much to make things right.

As the grandmother took her seat on one of the big stones, she smiled, resting the tiny pipe on her lap. This was a happy occasion, and the joy of her recollections and of the possibilities before her made her smile.

Yet the idea of sharing one's life with another in the companionship of marriage required her most serious consideration and personal reflection. So she closed her eyes, took a deep breath, and made a conscious connection with her mind and heart to All That Is and to All That Was and to All That Will Ever Be. This was her way of connecting to the Mystery.

Then she spoke, pausing now and then to breathe and to find the right words for another generation trying to walk the Path of Beauty.

"Among the old ways — somewhat shrouded in the mists of memories, and seen over many cycles, many seasons — remain the ceremonies," she began.

She opened her eyes and reached for a stick lying next to her on the ground. She tucked her dress in close to her knees, and leaned forward and drew a circle in the dirt.

"A marriage is a union," she said, scratching a line across the center of the circle. "A marriage is having someone to share your life."

She drew another line intersecting the first. Now the Circle of Life was at her feet. "Balance," she whispered. "Paths crossing. Sacred union. Completeness. Do you see?" The two young people looked at the circle and nodded, understanding the symbol of the words.

"So a marriage ceremony is an affirmation of one's commitment to the other," the grandmother said. "It is an affirmation of love. It's when each partner tells the other, "I honor and respect the person you are. Thank you for sharing life's journey with me."

She traced over the circle with the crooked stick, still holding the little pipe in her other hand.

"Whether you decide on an elaborate celebration or on a more simple expression, the purpose of the ceremony is what matters." She stopped drawing and looked at her granddaughter, and then at the young man who was soon to be her granddaughter's husband. Then she looked at them as one.

She took a pinch of tobacco out of a pouch she kept in her dress pocket. As she filled her pipe, she continued to talk.

"Some weddings became special events when drums resounded the rhythms of life and songs echoed the hope of good fortune, and when people danced for the sheer expression of joy, for with the marriage could come birth, the promise of new life, and the hope that what is good in people will continue."

She reached into her pocket and pulled out a lighter. She flicked it a few times before it ignited, then lit her pipe.

"Many of the marriage ceremonies, large and small, used a pipe, for the pipe was the physical form of the words of love and honor between two people. And through the sacrifice of tobacco, their words would become the smoke, becoming one with all things, expressing love and promise that could not be taken back."

She puffed on the stem until smoke swirled from the bowl, her eyes squinting through the smoke at the granddaughter and the young man sitting across from her.

"And what about a give-away?" she asked. "That's when you honor those who've supported you and loved you. That's when you give away many of those things you acquired when you lived your lives apart from one another."

"In the old days," she said, "a man would often give away a lot of the things that belonged to him when he lived his life alone, and the woman who was to be his wife would do the same. So, what they would acquire together became part of the home they would create together." She puffed on the little pipe, and smoke rings floated up into the air — circles within circles.

"But it's all about spirit," she said, motioning with the little pipe. "It's all about standing in the light and warmth of one's open heart. It's about expressing gratitude."

She placed the pipe back in her lap. "It's the spirit of the ceremony that's most important," she said. "If that spirit expresses all this and reflects balance and respect, if that spirit is born out of two people who truly love one another, then what's important takes place when those two people stand side by side, maybe bound at the wrists by a special kind of cloth or by a strip of deerskin, or perhaps they're wrapped under a single blanket. And in this way, they exchange their heartfelt feelings toward one another with words — words and feelings that help make their union beautiful and enduring."

A crow circled and then perched on a limb of an old oak, not far away from the circle of stones, and off in the distance two doves cooed to each other from different branches of the same tree. The birds reminded her of something: She recalled the meaning and the power of a marriage stick.

"Sometimes," she said, "a man and woman were given a marriage stick of oak or hickory, and for all the good things that would happen to them, and for all the hard times when their marriage would be tested and their love would survive, they marked each experience with a notch in the marriage stick." She glanced down at the circle in the dirt and once again began tracing over it. It was as though the motion unraveled images of her own marriage stick, and of the many notches her husband had carved into it over time.

And then she told them stories passed down through the generations about how other kinds of marriages would occur. She said that one of the most common was when two people simply went off together, even for a short time, and when they returned, they set up house together. This act of eloping and coming back and creating a home for each other announced and served as a marriage too.

"That kind of marriage," she said, "doesn't start out with the blessings that a wedding can bestow, but it still stands as a marriage."

She told them that a marriage of love and respect was a blessing shared with special people: relatives and friends, young and old, whose purpose was to bring the spirit of their good hearts and warm support to witness the experience of the wedding.

"And of course," she said, "a celebration of that kind of marriage, as with nearly all ceremonies, ended with a feast."

She bent over and picked up another twig. This one she used to clean out the bowl of her pipe, carefully allowing the ashes to sprinkle in the center of the circle of stones, joining the ashes of so many other ceremonies. And after she had scraped the bowl clean, she began describing the ingredients of the feast.

"This kind of celebration might include some meat, to honor the gifts of the four-legged ones; and corn, to honor the gift of Corn Mother; wild rice or potatoes, maybe some squash or some kind of beans, to acknowledge the sustenance they have provided; and fruit, especially strawberries, for their gifts of passion and peace."

"Many marriages today still may include a pipe or a blanket or a marriage stick," she said, "or really anything that can be used to symbolize and help create a sacred union between two people."

She said that by caring for such special things over time, we mirror the care that must be shown to keep a marriage strong. And something treasured, like a wedding pipe, a wedding blanket, or a marriage stick, becomes a physical reminder of the love and commitment that began it all.

"Your grandpa and I were married wrapped in our wedding blanket," she said, looking at her granddaughter, who appeared especially beautiful at that moment. "I remember how my uncle draped it over our shoulders, and it was under that blanket where your grandpa and I made our vows to each other."

Her eyes remained fixed on her granddaughter, for the grandmother could see, as if for the first time, the beauty and strength of her own grandmother, and her mother, and even her daughter in the young woman who sat across from her listening.

"My uncle gave me that blanket," she said, "and we used it to be married under, and to sleep under, and to make love and dream under. . . ." Her voice trailed off as the words faded to images that twinkled and blurred, fading into time.

And as she spoke of sacred things that sparked an original flame and kept alive the fire of love, a tear welled up and made its way down her cheek. "These special things," she said, "can help us to remember the gratitude we need to acknowledge the experience of love."

"Know in your hearts," she said, "that no matter how two people choose to become companions, no traditional way requires a legal document that declares their marriage. None demands a state witness. None needs a mediator to stand between two people in love and the Great Holy Mystery."

Then she closed her eyes once again and spoke of what she was seeing at that moment in the darkness where the stars of Time and Hope remain bright and strong.

"For a union of marriage," she said, "is first formed when the eyes of the beholder meet those of the beloved, when a deep and old kind of knowing beckons two hearts that will be forever young. When the dreams and life events of two lovers intertwine, and when the feelings are right, the sacred union forms and takes place within the sacred Circle of Life."

She opened her eyes once again and looked at her granddaughter and future grandson sitting across the ash pit on the other side of the circle. Then she stood, still clutching her tiny pipe in her hand, and smiled at them and nodded.

"Be kind to each other," she said, as though speaking from all the generations before her, "for it's really such a short journey, after all." And she turned, stepped over the old stone, and headed back into her house.

When she was inside, she sat at the old oak table in the kitchen, cutting strawberries. Occasionally, she'd place one in her mouth, shut her eyes tight, and savor the sweet memories of love and marriage.

14

A CEREMONY OF MARRIAGE

Love Charm
(Ojibwa)

What are you saying to me?
I am arrayed like the roses
And as beautiful as they.

They stood together, a man and a woman, holding hands within the circle of wild oaks and sabal palms. A warm wind swept the sweet spring air around them into a gentle, loving force that tantalized their senses.

The light of a full moon, big and white against the night, cast long shadows that stretched from the base of the trees to the bare feet of the two people who stood at the center of this place. The shadows connected them to everything, like the spokes of a great wheel connect the center hub to the great circle of the rim. Above them, wrapped all around them, was a blanket of night and glistening stars.

He told her that he would honor and respect her, and that he would support her on this journey. He held out a strand of deep red silk, and tied his wrist to hers.

In this sacred time when they talked of their union, he acknowledged to her his shortcomings. At times he had been selfish, sometimes impatient. He thanked her for the patience she had shown, and for the patience she would need.

Then he looked into her eyes, so deeply that she could see into his heart, and he promised to her his love for as long as he could breathe.

Then he kissed her hand.

These words did not spring from a shallow pool, but from a place deep within his spirit being. The words helped him to bring into clearer form what he knew to be true. He knew it in the way the Sun knows its own heat, in the way the eagle knows the wind, in the way the body knows the soul.

He knew it would take his lifetime to show her the full meaning of his promise. He said these things to her while the trees listened, while the moon watched, and while the evening star witnessed.

She too expressed her love for him there, in the little circle of oaks and palms within the greater circles of the earth and the galaxy and the night. She too acknowledged her weaknesses, and she thanked him for the strength she felt she could draw from the love he gave to her.

Her life has more meaning now, she told him, now that he would share in it, in her hopes and dreams, in her joys and even the sorrows that would come. She was delighted that this man would accompany her along the way. He was her companion.

She told him that she too would honor him and respect him and that, for as long as they shared this journey, she would give her trust to him.

"You are my heart," she whispered, while the trees listened, while the moon could see, and while the evening star witnessed.

And so, it was done.

She slowly untied the strand of deep red silk fastened to their wrists and gently kissed his lips. Their journey together had begun.

15

DIVORCE: WHEN THE GARDEN GROWS NO MORE

A Woman's Song
(Ojibwa)

You are walking around
Trying to remember
What you promised,
But you can't remember.

I f you've ever watched a rose fade before it blossomed or seen a garden deprived of rain and dried up in the sun, if you've ever seen a
creek depleted of water or felt your own precious love for another
trickle through your fingers because you can't squeeze them tight
enough to stop it, then you have encountered the same stark reality
that is divorce.

When the seeds of a marriage don't take to the soil of the new garden, the roots don't grow very deep. The earth may have seemed right for planting; the seeds may have appeared healthy, but for some reason neither the earth nor the seeds could fulfill their roles and reach their potential. Something went wrong along the way, or something wasn't right to begin with. We wanted it to be right, and all our wanting could not make it so.

The surface of the garden might even show signs of promise and growth, but the roots beneath stretch shallow and untested. When the winds of adversity sweep through, they can blow away the dried-up promise of fruition.

Why?
(Ojibwa)

Come,
I beseech you,
let us sing.
Why are you offended?

Sometimes, we simply don't know what is wrong. Perhaps the seeds of our garden require too much care, more than we can give without depleting ourselves. Perhaps the soil receives too little shade or not enough sun; perhaps we receive too little love and give too much. This season, the garden that is marriage may just not have been right for the seeds of promise.

The most difficult kind of divorce is when the seeds of marriage have been fruitful, and there are children playing in the garden. Everything should be done to assure these children that they are not at fault in any way, and that they are still loved and cherished. Decisions about property and possessions are secondary; the welfare of the children is primary. For children must know that both parents love them, and that they belong with the one parent who can best meet their need for a loving home, while the other parent remains strong in his or her love for the children and shows this through ongoing support and devotion.

In the old times, the children of divorce almost always stayed with their mother or their mother's family. When a husband and wife set up a home together that was not previously the property of either one, the home belonged to the mother and the children, for she owned the garden. All a man would leave with would be his personal belongings.

The Lover Who Went Away
(Ojibwa)

A loon I thought it was,
But it was
My love's
Splashing oar.

He has departed.
My love
Has gone on before me.
Never again
Can I see him.

Divorce, like death, is the end of something, and there is a grieving time when sorrow turns to mourning for what was, what might have been, and what will be no more.

Yet the death of a relationship, like the death of someone we love, can transcend into great change, change that is necessary for growth, change that leads to a better way of life, guided by a deeper wisdom — and this may lead us some day to another garden where our seeds of promise will reach beautiful fruition.

When I Think of Him
(Ojibwa)

Although he said it
Still
I am filled with longing
When I think of him.

We cannot control the love another feels. We can only know our own hearts. Divorce forces us to let go of the illusion of control and to acknowledge the stark reality of something that just cannot be. Resolving and dissolving what was but is no longer a marriage is yet another way of the heart, a way that can teach us how to love one another, and how to love ourselves.

Perhaps in time we can even learn to smile at our attempt at the journey of marriage. Perhaps it will make way for another that will come.

Or perhaps we will retain the memory in our hearts, and look back at what could have been . . . at what might have been . . . and . . .

At some future time

you will think of me
and cry. . . .

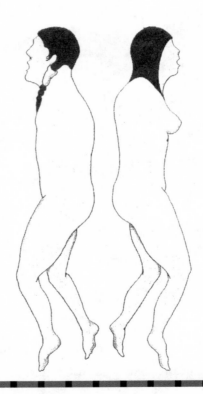

16

A CEREMONY OF REFLECTION

Carefully, with slow, precise movements, she places tiny cowry shells in a circle one by one on the shore. The hot sun is coming down on her shoulders. It is the same in this moment as it had been in the distant reach of her childhood recollection, when she remembers another divorce.

It was summer then too, and she was playing on the tire swing that hung from the old elm in her backyard. She had just been asked who she wanted to stay with, who she wanted to live with. . . . Mom? Or Dad? She remembers being asked pointblank by her mother. She remembers this now, while squatting on the shore in the heat of the sun.

It is a conscious ritual, in the heat of the summer sun: the gathering of the sacred cowry shells, creating the circle, the blessing of the sea. It is all part of a conscious design that sprang from her innermost being, from the unconscious yearning to understand herself, to know why she has become the person she is, here, now, as the waves crash close by.

Back then, it was as though her world as she knew it was crashing down around her. If she could have answered honestly, she would have preferred to stay with her dad. This she knows now as a young woman, placing another shell in the wet sand. But at that moment, as a little girl on a swing in her backyard, all her feelings of love and loyalty were tossing inside her like these waves on the windblown sea before her.

She had felt a strong connection to her dad — one that she retained throughout his life — but she also felt the loyalty bond with her mother, and with the rest of her brothers and sisters who were too young to choose. In the heat of the summer sun, she remembers how she couldn't say what she felt then because it would have hurt her mom's feelings too much. It's something she recognizes now as a life-long pattern for each of them, trying to guess what the other was thinking and feeling.

She had always been like her father, intelligent, temperamental, she recalls, and now she is doing something she thinks that even her mother had done as well: putting tiny shells in a circle in the sand.

She is so much older now than she was that hot day in July when she was asked to choose between loving Mom and loving Dad. As a little girl she could never understand why, if she loved them both, they couldn't be together, what had happened that they couldn't love each other anymore.

Perhaps it isn't until now, as her own marriage dissipates into the salty blue air, when she lays the last cowry shell in the sand, that she can feel she has gone full circle. She has completed the cycle of this awareness, and now she can begin the healing with the understanding born from this ceremony of reflection, even now while she watches the waves wash in with the tide and over the circle of the cowry shells.

As the sea carries her prayer-thoughts away, she stands a woman in the heat of the mighty Sun, and feels the salty spray on her face. Beyond her, toward the horizon, she notices a thin white haze has formed over the water.

It all seems so long ago, she thinks, and she gazes out at that sacred place where the sky and water and time transcend, so misty in the sea of memory.

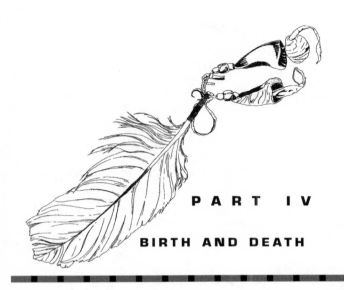

PART IV

BIRTH AND DEATH

It is the spirit of Cosmic Change,
the eternal growth that returns upon itself
to produce new forms.
It recoils upon itself like the dragon,
the beloved symbol of the Taoists.
It folds and unfolds as the clouds.

— Kakuza Okakura,
The Book of Tea

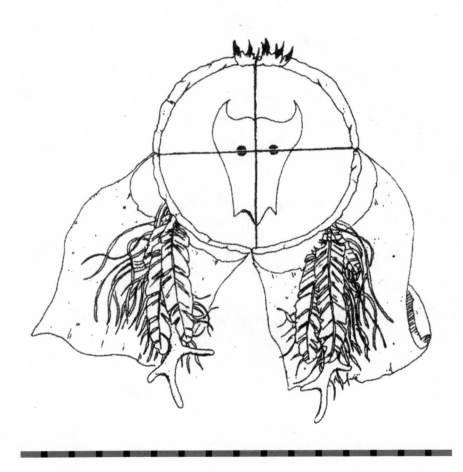

17

OMAHA PRAYER PRESENTING
AN INFANT TO THE WORLD

Ho! Ye Sun, Moon, Stars,

    All ye that move in the heavens,

        I bid you hear me!

Into your midst has come a new life.

      Consent ye, I implore!

Make its path smooth,

    That it may reach the brow of the first hill!

Ho! Ye Winds, Clouds, Rain, Mist,

    All ye that move in the air,

        I bid you hear me!

Into your midst has come a new life.

Consent ye, I implore!
Make its path smooth,
That it may reach the brow of the second hill!

Ho! Ye Hills, Valleys, Rivers, Lakes, Trees, Grasses,
All ye of the earth,
I bid you hear me!
Into your midst has come a new life.
Consent ye, I implore!
Make its path smooth,
That it may reach the brow of the third hill!

Ho! Ye Birds, great and small,
That fly in the air,
Ho! Ye Animals, great and small,
That dwell in the forest,
Ho! Ye Insects that creep among the grasses
And burrow in the ground,
I bid you hear me!
Into your midst has come a new life.
Consent ye, I implore!

Make its path smooth,
      That it may reach the brow of the fourth hill!

Ho! All ye of the heavens, all ye of the air,
      All ye of the earth,
            I bid you all to hear me!
Into your midst has come a new life.
      Consent ye, consent ye all, I implore!
Make its path smooth,
      Then shall it travel beyond the four hills!

18

THE CHILDREN, ALWAYS THE CHILDREN

She said that she knew the moment of conception. She described the feeling like the sunlight touching her skin.

He said he was aware of that instant because he felt the spirit of his own being fall into hers. It was as though their spirits had merged in order to create. And they became in that twinkle of time as one . . . when two humans fulfill their part in creation.

The conception extended beyond anything sensual and sexual; it happened intentionally, so what is good about them as people would live on . . . so the vision of seeing oneself in relation to the totality of the universe would yet again bring benevolence and peace . . . so their faith in the Old Ways of regarding life would continue.

While the spirit of her child takes physical form in her womb, she begins to pass on to the child and to all those around her what she knows to be beautiful. For she has summoned, she has come to embody, the spirit of the Earth's *orenda*. And it comes to her in familiar ways and yet in newer, more exciting ways as well.

She hears more clearly now the gentle breezes of spring whispering through the outstretched limbs of the great redwoods or stirring the boughs of the tall pines. Her senses heighten, and she grows more aware of the energy and power now when the lightning cracks and the Thunderers boom and the wild winds whirl in a summer's storm.

Now, in new ways, she feels that sound, she senses that energy, and becomes more conscious of all the vibrations and sensations outside herself that she and her unborn child are exposed to. So she seeks the company of the good-hearted people and the peaceful places of the earth. She wants to participate more in ceremonies of love and thanksgiving — and the medicine people encourage her presence because they feel that such influence on the unborn child is important and that a pregnant woman during these sacred occasions attracts good spirits to the circle.

During this time when human life takes form within her, she also tries to seek the special places on the land that bring her closer to the natural sounds of the earth. The beach draws her to the shore, where the movement of the ocean as the waves break and wash toward her helps soothe the stirring forces of life within her, and helps to acquaint that new life with the natural rhythms of the world and of the universe.

And when she must go into the midst of the world, with its crowds and technologies, she becomes more conscious of people and the way they speak and the things they say, for the vibrations of spoken words may in some mysterious way be felt by the unborn forming miraculously inside her womb. The elders say we may never know for certain what the unborn within the womb learns during the developing stages, but that it is not worth the risk to treat the unborn child any other way than we would want to treat the child after the birth.

As a mother now, she wants to be wise and protective in these ways, and at times has to remove herself from negative or harmful conversations, or other uncomfortable situations.

So much of the attention of both the mother and the father

focuses on the development of their unborn child. The words of the elders echo throughout their lives, forever reminding all those who follow them: the children, always the children.

Like the mother, the father can share what he knows of Beauty's Way as well. He may beat the rhythms of life on his deerskin drum, or serenade this new spirit with the melodies of the flute, or shake the sounds of male and female rain with his turtle shell rattle. With any instrument he chooses, including his own voice, he speaks with music, lovingly and peacefully, to their unborn child.

He wants so much to emulate the beneficial and beautiful things of this earth, so he may cut and shape, or just provide, a cradle board or some other well-crafted device to secure and keep comfortable this new life, for the infant will be coming from the peaceful and cozy world of the womb.

Mother and father do these things to help influence the life of the one who is yet to be born. They do these things because they want to keep alive the old proven ways of seeing and living in this world. They do these things in the belief that they will help the child walk the Path of Beauty.

They do these things because they recognize the enormous responsibility for bringing a new life into this world. For they are the keepers of the faith, and no greater affirmation can there be than the birth of their child.

19

THE SILENT PLACES OF THE HEART

Like a trail of starlight stretched across an ocean of time and memory, a young mother begins tracing her own path of origin that leads to the heavens, and reconnects herself in mind and spirit with the universe she is a part of. Now pregnant with life, she feels her relationship to this Great Holy Mystery through the gentle flutter and subtle movement of her unborn child. And her relationship with the Earth grows stronger. So does her connection with the Moon.

One morning, she rises and greets the morning star. Another day, she relaxes in the rays of a noonday sun. And on special nights, she basks in the white light of the Moon. For now she seeks the silent places of the heart, where she can rest with her newly forming child, and recount to it the beauty that is the Mother who sustains us all, the beauty of the Father who protects us. She speaks to her child of the Power of the mighty Sun. She speaks prayers of Thanksgiving to the beautiful Moon.

Her mate remains, in some way, never removed from the process and its power. He feels the yearning of his heart as well, and knows that great change has enveloped his life too. So he makes time to sit alone and reconnect to the life he has lived, and wonder about his new life to come. He too speaks words of gratitude in advance for the strength of body and spirit he must have in his unfamiliar role as a father, for the patience he will need, for the sacrifices he will make.

As the wind sweeps around him, he stands in the direction of the Rising Sun and releases the fear that so often accompanies change. In the presence of the light and heat of the Sun, he accepts the fire of his primary purpose.

Both together and apart, this woman and man, these parents of an unborn child, acknowledge their love for Earth and Sky, and address the great powers of the Sun and Moon. The responsibility they have assumed humbles them, for these human parents know in their hearts that they are only the caretakers — that the Earth, the Sky, the Sun, and the Moon are the real parents and grandparents of this new life, and of all life within this circle they know as their world.

Magical and sacred becomes the cycle, magical because of its extraordinary power, sacred because it is regarded with reverence. This mother of the People serves with a good heart as a creatriss of life itself, and in some innate way she feels that everything she does, and everything she thinks, influences the child that will be born into this world, even as her ancestral memory flows in the child's blood.

At no other stage of this new life will she have such influence, for now the unborn child remains an extension of herself. She controls what her child hears, what her child eats, even what her child feels. She knows that once this new life passes through the tunnel of birth and breathes its first breath of air, that child will be separate from her, a life unto itself. It will be a separation that will help prepare her for others that may come.

All that she does now, and all that her mate can do, will not ensure the goodness of the child's life, or its longevity. Mother and father retreat to the silent places of the heart to gain the strength necessary to give birth, and then to guide the child in the world to the best of their abilities.

They retreat to the silent places of the heart to remember the spirits, forever present, who dwell within the Mystery.

They pray to remember, always, the Great Holy Mystery.

20

RETURNING THE PLACENTA:
A STORY OF GRATITUDE

The wintry March wind sweeping across the icy Mississippi does not discourage her journey down to its snowy shore. She is a determined teenage mother, bundled up in bulky winter clothes. Because she has chosen no mate for herself, she follows close behind her sister's husband, whom she has asked to help her return the placenta.

With one hand she reaches out for bare tree branches for balance, and with her other she holds onto the tiny prayer bundles. Just ahead, he carries a shovel over his shoulder and, tucked under his arm, a plastic jar that contains the placenta.

She knew that a trek on a winter's day down such a winding, slippery path required help; perhaps she didn't fully realize how such a journey reflected meaning in her own life.

It had been a month since she gave birth to her son. The night before, under a waxing crescent Moon, she brought her brother-in-law a pouch filled with a traditional blend of tobacco and red willow bark, and asked if he would help her now, at the beginning of this new cycle.

She had accompanied him down this trail once before, when he and her older sister had carried the placenta that nourished their baby down to the river's shore. Spring had come early that year, and the earth was moist from melted snow. The maples and oaks and elms had just started to bloom, and she saw the new buds, so vulnerable to the winter chill, open for the first time to the sun. She wondered now if perhaps those trees were a sign of her own primary Purpose fulfilled so soon.

She remembered, when her sister had given birth, her sister's husband had asked the doctor and nurses to save the placenta, and they did as they were requested, placing it in a plastic container. When her sister returned from the hospital, they put the container in the refrigerator. Then they made four tobacco ties, cutting little squares of colored cloth, placing a pinch of tobacco in each, along with a prayer, and securing each one with sinew.

In this way they made four little bundles, one for each of the Four Directions — yellow, red, black, and white. They did this as an offering for their new son, to help secure a life journey that would take him beyond the Four Hills.

> *Into your midst has come a new life.*
> *Consent ye, consent ye all, I implore!*
> *Make its path smooth,*
> *Then shall it travel beyond the four hills!*

Her sister had told her then what the elders had taught long ago about bringing new life into the world, and how doing these things helped ensure its survival during that first precarious year.

The elders said that the placenta that provided the child with sustenance in the womb is sacred for that reason, and should be given back to Mother Earth, who provides for all her children. They said the placenta contains all that is necessary to sustain life, so in a spirit way it is of the Earth and should be returned to her with prayers of

Thanksgiving, not only for what Mother Earth has already given, but for all that she will give to all men and women, and their children's children for as long as they live.

The elders instructed each generation of mothers and fathers to find a special, private place in the woods, or somewhere like this spot, along the shore of the wide Mississippi, to bury the placenta. In this way the Earth reclaims what is hers, and the natural processes continue undisturbed by humans.

In this way they create a sacred place where a teenage mother now stands over a hole dug by her brother-in-law, and watches him release the crimson placenta from the container. As it falls deep into the ground, she drops her little prayer ties to rest alongside it, while she speaks words of gratitude for the gift of her child's life and for all the gifts from the source that had sustained him in her body and continues now to sustain him in the world.

Then they go down to the river, and watch the waters catch the specks of tobacco she sprinkles, with more prayers of Thanksgiving. The river flows cold and strong in the currents beneath the cracked ice, traveling South toward the salt water womb of the Earth.

21

THE RITUALS OF NAMES

I open my eyes to your dawn,
I open my arms to embrace the beauty of your new day,
I open my heart for the new life that stirs within me.
Can you hear the beating of our two hearts?
Grant me a name, Gitchie Manido!
For my child I seek a name.

To see an animal in a dream. To take special notion of a certain star. To observe the phases of the moon. All this embraces the ritual of a name.

The caress of a summer breeze. The petals of a rose. The kiss of the sunlight at dawn.

A loon's echo across the still waters of a lake. The leaves of a white oak rustling in autumn. The breath of a dolphin.

All this embraces the ritual of a special name.

Prayer and contemplation. Dreams and observation. As the unborn forms within her womb, the mother prepares for the welcoming of this new life. She wants this new life to remember, and help her and others remember, our human connection to the universe and to the earth. She wants this new life to have the power that a good name can give, and the connection to the natural world that she feels so much a part of. She wants the guidance that a good name may provide.

She stands in the backyard with both hands holding her swollen belly, and she says softly to the Mystery, *"Grant me a name for my child."*

It is late in the morning. The sunlight streams through the branches of the old maples that stretch and reach out above her. The last falling leaves of autumn rain colors down upon her. And deep within, she feels a kind of swirling sensation, like the tiny gust that suddenly sweeps around her. It is as though her unborn child stirs too, in a way that she can't explain, except to know that the movement itself affirms her prayer. She senses a conscious awareness growing within her, a living part of her, yet a life separate from her own being.

Throughout the afternoon she sits on a rug on the living room floor and works on a coffee table, all the while contemplating a name while she cuts and forms the leather for a new tobacco pouch.

Toward evening she thinks more about a name while she peels and cuts potatoes for supper. She thinks about it while she slices carrots, and snaps green beans with her fingers.

During dinner she speaks about it, and before she goes to bed she gazes out her bedroom window, thinking about it until her eyes fix on a single white star. It seems so unusually bright that it beckons her to examine it more closely. She stands, leaning slightly, her cheek gently pressed against the cold glass, contemplating this particular star — and then she feels as if she's looking through a kind of portal into another reality.

She closes her eyes slowly, and wonders about the name her child will be known by. She opens them again and gazes once more at the white star. She concentrates on it, and makes a silent prayer, asking about the name. In her mind single words and fragmented thoughts float like pollen dust tossed into the night air.

"Strength and gentleness," she whispers. "He must be strong like the deer," she says, "for there is also gentleness in such a being." Then she speaks as quietly as the autumn leaves falling on the roof. "He must be good-hearted," she says.

She wants a name that connects her child to the Sky, to the Earth, and to the Mystery. She wants a name that will help guide her child on the Path of Beauty.

As she lays her head on her pillow, she wonders some more about a name, and her thoughts carry her into dreamtime. Maybe there, the spirits will speak to her. Maybe there, in the world of that other reality, she will be given an understanding that will help her on this quest for a name.

"Thank you," she says softly, day after day, night after night, even as the cool autumn winds turn wintry. During this time she realizes that an undertaking such as finding a name can involve a great many things and a good deal of consideration, even though she knows that the name she chooses for her child may change as the child changes. But she also knows that, in these times especially, the one name she places on the certificate of birth will more than likely remain with her child through a lifetime. So she must choose thoughtfully and wisely.

During the last days of the fall, she considered naming her child after one of her great-aunties or uncles, but she was reminded then of the story of how Crazy Horse received his name, and of how in many cultures you couldn't pass on a name that belonged to someone else unless there was good reason or unless the person wanted it passed on. She recalled that it was the father of Crazy Horse who passed on his own name to his son, and then, it has been said, his father took the name Worm. How humble, she thought, as she watched the last of the falling leaves float to the earth.

And then there was the issue of which language the name would be, and if it were in a language other than English, there was the matter of pronunciation. She wanted a name with a sound that most people could speak without much difficulty, for this might help make the road a little easier for her child who must live in, or at least be exposed to, this civilized world of English-speaking schools and jobs and English legal documents.

Later on, when her child grows to become an adult, a vision quest may lead him or her to another name, or a powerful and sacred dream might reveal a new name. Or perhaps, after being observed by others, this young woman's child may grow to earn a new name, one given by relatives or friends.

By whatever means or ways her baby acquires a name now, it will one day, no doubt, mirror the character and personality, and voice and echo the reputation, of that person. A good name at birth can serve as a guiding force on the journey that is this life. A good name can become a source of great strength while living in this great Wheel of Life.

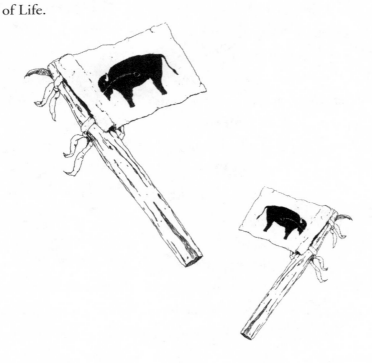

2 2

SHE REQUESTS A NAME

An old man once said,
In the end, when your name is spoken,
the sentiment evoked by its vibration
will show how well
you have lived your life.

He was about to become a great-uncle. The little niece whose name he had dreamed before she was born had grown to become a beautiful young woman and would soon be giving birth to her own child. Now, just as her mother had done when she was born, she went to her great-uncle and gave him a new tobacco pouch filled with precious tobacco descended from a plant generations old. Then she asked him if he would help her find a good name for her child.

He loosened the pouch and reached in with his fingers and removed a pinch of the shredded dried leaves. "If I were you," he said, as he sniffed it, savoring the aroma, "I'd take some of this tobacco and make an offering to the spirit world."

He got up from where he sat on the front porch and walked a few steps to his little garden. As he squatted close to the plants, he felt a warm feeling wash over him, like the sunlight rising on a summer day, only now the warmth poured into his heart, even into his soul. To be loved and respected so much by his beautiful niece made all the struggles he had endured to hold on to the old ways surely worth it. He felt one cycle completing itself — and yet others still unfolding.

He closed his eyes and sprinkled the tobacco over the earth around the plants in his garden. The tobacco was sacrificed to the plants for this prayer, so it had to be a strong prayer, a meaningful one, not filled with a lot of meandering words, but a prayer that was respectful and clear and concise.

And so, his prayer was short — may I help find a good name, a name of hope for this new child of the future and the universe, this new baby of his beautiful niece.

His eyes remained shut while he made the offering and sounded the words of his prayer, and he journeyed into his soul, into that

familiar part of him that is spirit, where he could see and hear the relatives of his distant past, the ones who had encouraged him when he
was young and searching — the ones he had loved and who had loved
him along the way.

And though they were separated by time and worlds, he could see
them with his eyes closed tightly and he could hear their ghost voices
speaking to him out of the place of spirit. They spoke from his memories, out of the Mystery.

With his eyes still shut, he addressed his young niece.

"Pay attention to the natural world and to the things of that
world. Seek council with your ancestors. Appeal to the Great Mystery.
Talk with those elders who can still speak the old language and who
still believe in the old ways."

Then he opened his eyes and looked at her. The long strands of
her crow-black hair glistened. Her ivory skin, the warmth of her dark
eyes, the pretty smile of her rose-colored lips all captivated him. She
was a treasure to behold. In her beauty he could see generations into
the future. In her beauty he could see hope. In her beauty he could see
an abundance of love.

During the winter solstice ceremony, when the air was still and cold and crisp, when Mother Earth was in her dreamtime, he first saw the star, an unusually bright one. He tried to remember if he had ever seen it before. It stood out among the others because it was so much larger and appeared as white as fresh sparkling snow, rather than a shiny silver. And it didn't twinkle like the others; it floated big and constant. It was as though this one star had reached out to him and touched him in a way no other star ever had.

It wasn't until he got home the following dawn that he knew that the name he had been asked to find had something to do with that star. He knew it the way clouds know the rain, the way trees know the wind, the way the pipe knows the smoke.

Many miles away, as she drove home from a family gathering, a white light suddenly flared across the sky in front of her. The light streaked from one end of the windshield to the other in the blink of an eye. But it also shot across her mind, illuminating it, vanquishing the shadows of fear and uncertainty that hid in the recesses, ready to haunt her quiet times, and her sleep. As the white star shot across the sky, her whole body ignited, every cell stirring in the rush of excitement and anticipation that went through her.

What was that? she said to herself. The words were more of a reaction than a question needing an answer, accepting that she could never really know for certain the mystery of such things. Still, her eyes searched the sky wondrously and her hands gripped the steering wheel as if it were the Wheel of Life itself.

When her son was born toward the end of winter, she called him Ska Ahnung (White Star), or Ahnung, a child of a star, and he is the hope and faith for the future of a good-hearted people.

23

CHILD OF THE CORD

The young woman sat cross-legged on an Indian blanket on the living room floor. Her new baby lay in front of her, becoming aware of his new senses. The elder uncle of the young mother sat rocking in a chair alongside of them.

Suddenly all the energy focused on the infant's belly, as the young mother softly touched the area around her son's umbilical cord. She paused and then, ever so carefully, she moved the cord, testing its connection. Then she gently pulled it, and released it from the baby.

It seemed to fall into her hand. And it seemed, too, that all this had happened before.

It was at this moment that the spirit of past generations stirred within the old uncle, and he too paused. As he watched his niece dressing with broad, smooth leaves the place that was now the infant's navel, he felt he had been given a great gift, a new sense of purpose, one that only comes with age and wisdom.

He slowly resumed his rocking, and began to talk to his niece about the turtles and the lizards, about the pouches and the bundles, and about the sacred meaning of the cord.

"When your son was born and we cut the umbilical cord," he said, "your child became a tiny life form unto himself." He rocked back and forth, and watched the slender fingers of his niece place the tiny knot on the blanket alongside her baby. Her son was now separated from her, a unique being, a child of the Mystery.

The uncle stopped rocking and looked at the little one, who lay upon a pretty robe, his tiny feet and hands touching the air, his glassy black eyes reflecting the sunlight that streamed through the frost and the blinds on the windows. He was so small and helpless, this little one, and yet he was the biggest part of their lives.

"He's completely dependent and vulnerable," the old uncle said.

"And that's what calls out to me, and to all those who are his relatives."

As he spoke, she wrapped her new son securely in a small red and blue blanket, warm wool woven into colorful geometric patterns by his aunts and given to the infant at his birth. Then she loosened a couple of her buttons and opened her blouse just enough to press her tiny son to her breast. She relaxed and listened. . . .

The old uncle shut his eyes, to see deeper and more clearly the things of the heart, and resumed his rocking and his retelling of the stories and of the meanings still connected to the cord.

He told her that it would be good to do certain things to help ensure that a good person would now inhabit this world: one who would contribute to the creative force of the Mystery, one who would respectfully embrace the beauty of the world — of Mother Earth — and one whose own power of goodness would help him live a long and meaningful life.

He told her that sometime ago the old ones had said the cord that was still attached to the placenta was to be returned to the earth with the placenta, but the piece of cord with the tiny knot that was attached to the infant's belly required a different kind of attention. He said that this part of the cord is very important and very sacred. He told her the People had believed long ago that the cord of the newborn remains linked to its wellbeing, especially during the first tenuous year of life.

"The cord retains some kind of connection," he said, "not only to the realm of the spirit, but to the identity of the child." He said that an older woman, "a grandmother many times," had told him what can happen to children whose cords were not properly cared for — "they can become adults who have lost their connection to spirit, and are always searching for something."

He spoke these words with the certainty of generations.

The young mother turned her little son toward her other breast, and whispered his name and stroked his downy dark hair with her fingertips. How good he felt in her arms! Protected and loved. But she couldn't push away other thoughts that made her shiver inside — what about the times when he would not be cuddled close to her?

She remembered stories of babies who died mysteriously in their sleep, and of those who had grown too sick and weak to continue a long life's journey. She thought about all those humans whose twisted nature compels them to steal away the beauty and innocence of this world.

"How can I protect him, Uncle?" she said, her soft voice shaking.

Her uncle had sensed her uneasiness and insecurity even before she spoke. He too had felt the same pangs of fear for her when she was a baby, wanting to protect her innocence and beauty with his life.

"There are ways," he said. His dark eyes were shining behind half-closed lids. He didn't want to fully open them, for he was seeing in two worlds. He saw his beautiful niece nursing her firstborn child, and he saw the shadows and the ever-changing forms of things in the space of his mind. "That's why we must care for the cord," he said. "And that's where the turtle comes in."

The girl adjusted the baby in her arms, and flicked the silky strands of her hair that fell luxurious down her back. Her uncle gazed at her through his narrowed eyes.

Yet, even as he looked at her, he also looked inward, and saw generations of women in her beauty, and heard generations in her gentle words, for women through the ages had also embraced their newborn children and had once spoken their words of concern. Every female line down to her had given birth, and each one had wished for a long and meaningful life for her child.

He closed his eyes once again and rocked farther back, as if he were about to launch himself through that Time and Space where memories dwell. He rocked back and forth, back and forth, and reached into the deep recesses of his mind for the stories he'd been told about the calico bundles and deerskin pouches that protected the cord. Eyes closed, he could see the turtle designs, cut and woven, colorful and strong, and the brightly beaded lizards.

"Tell me, Uncle," she said. "Tell me about the bundles and pouches." She had been watching him rocking with his eyes closed, seeing things that she could only imagine. "Tell me more about the turtle designs, and the shiny lizards."

It felt good to him knowing he had something to share, something to pass on to someone who wanted to know. He was keeping something sacred alive. This was his purpose now. And yet, his respect for his niece and for the things of the past that he knew, and his reluctance to impose on her any of his own ideas of what was good for the child, all caused him to carefully consider his motives and his timing, and especially his choice of words.

"Tell me more, Uncle. Please."

He stopped rocking and looked at her. "The power of these things, once we see it," he said quietly, "is just as obvious as knowing we need the air to breathe, and knowing that air has the power to fill us with life."

He pushed the old rocking chair back and forth again, moving from past to present. "Generations of your ancestors believed in these things," he said. "And they always tried to do the best for the children. They tell us about the courage of the turtle. They knew about the tenacity of the lizard's will to survive." He slowed the rocker, but did not stop. "Let the ancestors guide us now," he said. "You are here because those who cared for you followed the sacred ways. Now your newborn's life requires that same kind of love."

Without even looking he could see the young woman before him, nursing the infant who was his great-nephew. And he could feel the presence of loving generations guiding him as he went on to speak more of these things of the past, all the while admiring this image of beauty before him.

He told her that the turtle shell had once recorded the passing of our moons. He said that everything about the turtle connects us to life in natural Time. As she lifted her baby to her shoulder and began gently patting his back, the old uncle became aware that he was really speaking to both of them, mother and child, and he began telling them about the protective power in the spirit of the turtle's shell. He told them about the strength of courage that dwells within the turtle's heart.

"Imagine," he said, "the light of a full moon glowing on a golden beach. Imagine the sand slowly stirring with tiny creatures crawling from their mother's nest, ten, twenty, fifty, hundreds. Imagine...."

And then he described how the baby turtles scramble toward the sea, gesturing as he spoke, and how some of them slip as they scratch their way up the small sandy mounds, and fall on their backs, and can't turn over. He told them how other tiny turtles head off in the wrong direction, confused, sometimes toward the artificial lights of beach houses or hotels. "These poor little ones," he said, "often wander off never to be seen again."

The old uncle slowed his rocker to a halt and opened his eyes. It was as though he was coming out of a trance. He saw his niece looking up at him, holding her baby close. It felt so good for her to hold him close. "What about the ones that make it, Uncle?" she said. "Surely some must make it."

He smiled and nodded slowly. "Yes, my girl, some of them have to make it."

And she knew why he said that in the way that he did. "Because the species has to continue," she said. And she heard the echo of her uncle's words, and it became an incantation she'd whisper in the days ahead. Some of them have to make it.

The infant burped, and they laughed — somehow it was a great, resounding affirmation of life. "And the ones that do make it to the water," he said, "have a chance of surviving that first year. But to do it, they need all the power they were born with, and some good luck along the way."

He watched his niece trace with her finger a turtle shell around the cord that lay on the blanket, and he pushed himself forward and began to rock once more. And as he rocked, he told her a story. It wasn't a pleasant story, and he was reluctant to tell it, but the story made a good point. He said that his grandfather had once found a turtle that had been run over by a car. His grandfather told him that the old turtle's heart continued to beat, long after it was dead. The uncle then said that her new son would need a strong heart too — that it would take a strong heart to walk the Path of Beauty in this life. "It will take the power of a turtle's heart," he said.

The slant of the morning light that had poured into the room shifted and changed with the old uncle's stories into an afternoon glow. The infant slept without stirring in a cradle board, wrapped in the cocoon of his colorful robe. A dream catcher dangled just in front of him from the strip of curved cedar that protected his precious little face and head. His mother sat beside him and worked carefully with a pair of scissors in one hand and a piece of deerskin in the other. Slowly and deliberately she cut out the shape she had sketched on it while listening to her uncle, the shape of a turtle.

Over the years, she would listen to her inner voice, and often hear the words of her uncle. She cared well for her baby, and had designed and cut and beaded a beautiful pouch with shiny lizard patterns that served as a decoy for the mischievous and malevolent spirits that are easily distracted by the glitter of beauty. "They're the spirits that chase the illusion," her old uncle had told her.

She put the cord in a simple deerskin pouch, along with some sweet scented sage, a small strand of braided sweetgrass, and shavings of red cedar. On the base of the pouch, she beaded in green a turtle swimming upward.

Years later he would lay the beaded bundles on the new Indian blanket alongside his young wife, as her fingers tenderly touched the cord of the tiny baby who lay before them in the same way his mother had touched his cord. And he would know that the things of this ceremony had all happened before, in so many ways, in countless times. And the unconscious memories would rise out of the pools of sun and shadows like morning mist, take form, and swirl ghostlike within him.

24

ZUÑI PRAYER PRESENTING AN INFANT TO THE SUN

Now this is the day.
Our child,
Into the daylight
You will go out standing.
Preparing for your day,
We have passed our days.

When all your days were at an end,
When eight days were past,
Our sun father
Went to sit down at his sacred place.
And our night fathers,
Having come out standing to their sacred place,
Passed a blessed night.
Now this day,
Our fathers, dawn priests,
Have come out standing to their sacred place,
Our sun father
Has come out standing to his sacred place.
Our child, it is your day.
This day,
The flesh of the white corn, prayer meal,
To our sun father
This prayer meal we offer.

May your road be fulfilled.
Reaching to the road of your sun father,
When your road is fulfilled,

In your thoughts may we live,

May we be the ones your thoughts will embrace,

For this, on this day,

To our sun father,

We offer prayer meal.

To this end:

May you help us all to finish our roads.

25

WHAT IS LIFE? WHAT IS DEATH?

*That which the children of the earth
do not comprehend as they travel
the roads of the earth
becomes clear to them only when
they have passed on to the great mysteries
in Wah'kon-tah.*

What is life? It is the flash of a firefly on a summer's night. It is a pinch of dust tossed to the wind. It is the buffalo's breath on a cold day. It is the single beat of a pulsar from the outer limits of the Milky Way. It is an instant, the flicker of a sparrow's wing.

"Only the Sky and Earth will last long," the old man sang. Only Sky and Earth, and the Sun, Moon, and the stars will be here when everything else is gone.

You and me? In the great Totality that is the universe, in the great Circle of Life that extends beyond our capacity to fully imagine, we are interrelated to all things that ever were and will ever be.

In the infinite wholeness that always was, without beginning and without end, we share this life, blessed with a conscious awareness, blessed with the magic of this human form, in whatever condition in which it exists, for a fleeting moment.

In the time it takes a star to shoot across the sky on a clear night, or a sudden gust of air to sweep across the sands of a windswept shore, a human life span comes and goes in the eternal expanse of spinning galaxies and black holes, of countless stars and celestial seas of space and light, inexplicable and unimaginable within this Great Holy Mystery. This is our brief reality.

It never quite feels that we have enough time on this earth, but it is all we have, and it may be all we really need. For, in the end, we continue to live on in the minds and hearts of the living and in the Oneness of all things. While life allows us the individual experience on this earth, death is the transition to Totality and the stars.

It has been said that the old ones never doubted the immortal nature of spirit, that indefinable something that animates us and gives us life, yet neither did they care to speculate on the state of that spirit in a future afterlife. They did not debate or contemplate the existence of a heaven and hell as reward and punishment for human behavior. They did not choose to consider reincarnation or the attainment of Nirvana, though they knew that in a universe that is boundless with potential and limitless with possibilities, it is all conceivable.

Yet they did pass down to us a great sense of spiritual contentment, for they believed that the spirit that the Great Mystery breathed into a human being returns to the One who gave it, and at death this spirit can hear our prayers, and can remain among the living for a while for the consolation of family and friends. It is said that once the spirit is freed from the body, it exists within all of nature.

What a wonderful idea, knowing that the spirit of the one we loved who has died dwells everywhere — and that it can be felt from time to time in the warmth of a summer breeze, or heard in the melody of a mockingbird's song, or seen in the beauty of a strand of pearls.

"Death?" the old man said. "There is no death, only a change of worlds."

26

A CEREMONY FOR DEATH

 Song Sung over a Dying Person
(Ojibwa)

You are a spirit,
I am making you a spirit,
In the place where I sit
I am making you a spirit.

The first ceremony after she crossed over was taking the clothes that she died in and burning them. That's what the elders said to do. Those things were part of her transition, and were not to remain.

Perhaps they could retain the memories of the sadness connected with death and sorrow. Perhaps the clothes would continue to evoke those feelings among the living. One thing was certain: fire was purification. And the clothes she had worn while she died came to be regarded sacred in some way.

Now it seemed that everything the old ones said to do at this time made some kind of sacred sense; every act seemed deliberate. Even crying had a purpose. "Cry for your loss," they said. "Do not cry for her. She is spirit now. She is one with the Mystery."

One of the sisters took the pajamas and the nightgown out to the fire that the husband's brother and younger male relatives had started. Everyone else had gathered there, in the backyard of their home. They all stood on the earth, some apart and alone, some huddled in small groups. It felt to all of them like the world had stopped, in some way. The air did not stir. The birds did not sing. Only the Sun moved, marking the passing of time.

And the people moved about too, slowly and quietly, until they each found their place in the circle around the fire. Some of them wept; some stared sorrowfully into the flames.

One of her brothers held a plate of tobacco before him and went from person to person offering it to them. They reached out and took a pinch to hold and to pray with. Once more the words of the elders softly carried from ear to ear, from heart to heart, reminding the People that the mourning was for the loved ones who are left behind, for the loss that each person in that circle was feeling, and not for the woman who has made the Great Change. *She is spirit now.... She is spirit.* So they spoke words of gratitude and encouragement and reassurance. "Thank you, dear sister," they said. "Thank you, dear friend. Thank you for the goodness you brought into my life."

And as they squeezed the tobacco in their hands between their fingers, they said, "Be strong in spirit now, sister. You will be missed so much. But everything will be okay. Your children will be cared for. . . ."

Then one by one the People placed their prayers with the tobacco into the fire with the burning bundle of clothes. While they did this, a man who was a warrior began beating on a drum. Then he and his wife, who was her dear friend, began singing an old song.

It felt right, the people in the circle thought, to leave this world with song. And the singing felt good to them too, for the old ones had said, "We are born into this world with song and we leave it with song."

The singing of this man and woman, this husband and wife, took the emotions of the People and expressed them through the song. How powerful it all was! And it felt as though the spirit of the woman who had died was there watching everything. It felt as though her spirit could hear the singing and the prayers of the people in the circle, and could see them rising in the fire and merging with her in the

Oneness of all things. The presence of her spirit made the People feel good. It comforted them. It consoled them.

Inside the house, in her bedroom where she died, the women closest to her in life helped to clean and dress the body of their beloved sister and friend. They put pretty beaded moccasins on her feet, and placed the eagle feather in her hands that was with her in the end. By her side, her husband and each child left something meaningful and beautiful.

That night the drumming began. Men brought their drums and their rattles, their sorrow and their love. They joined with her husband and her children and drummed and drummed and drummed. There was not a moment that night when the drums were silent. The beating brought strength to the heavy-hearted friends and family, and the sound of the beating could be felt in the Mystery and in the spirit that the woman had now become.

Perhaps the drumming attracts the spirits of those who have already crossed over, the relatives and ancestors. Perhaps it is the music that helps allow the spirit a chance to gather itself in a familiar place near the body and ready itself for its journey across the stars. It is said that our spirits will travel the celestial sea across the Milky Way.

And perhaps the beating drums reassure the spirit that life will continue for the living, and that the old ways will still continue.

But one thing is certain: the beating of the drums all night announces to the world that someone special has made the Great Change.

A few years before, when this woman was mourning the passing of her mother, her wise old uncle had told her that the way she dealt with her mother's death would be the way she would want her children to deal with hers — "because," he said, "all mothers die."

She remained by her mother's side when cancer claimed her life. She remained close by her mother when she transcended into spirit and became one with the Mystery. She stood alongside her mother's gravesite with family and friends, and was there to help encourage her mother's spirit to continue on its journey. She was there to help all of those in mourning to remember that her mother believed in the old ways.

Now her children prepared her for the same journey. Her ashes were returned to the earth, to her favorite places where she had lived and loved. Many people from all walks of life, young and old, came to show their respect to her family and lend their support in whatever ways they could. They came from everywhere and gathered in a great circle that honored this mother, this wife, this woman of the People who had died. In the center of this circle was a large hole with mounds of dirt piled around it and a young oak tree lying on its side, ready to be planted.

Many people brought colorful prayer ties, and others held pretty feathers. A young woman made a dream catcher. An old man carried strands of red peppers. An older woman who was a close friend, and her husband, had cut six strips of colorful ribbon, each color representing one of the Four Directions, the Sky, and the Earth.

They moved around the oak tree and loosely fastened their little offerings to its delicate branches.

When this was done, the departed woman's husband and children pulled the tree into the hole and, on their hands and knees, shoveled and pushed the earth back down until the hole was filled and the tree was planted. It would be a place they could return to, a place to meditate, to pray, and to remember. As the children and her husband stood near the tree and the rest of the people stood in a circle around them, the sunlight glistened on the tiny leaves and upon the colorful prayers and symbols of love that decorated its branches.

The old ones say, "When we die, we cross over." They say that it is important for the living to encourage the journey that is involved in that crossing over. "Persevere onward," they say, "to that peaceful place in the Mystery."

And so each person in the circle that day recalled what this woman had meant to them, and thanked her, but also encouraged her spirit to journey on, to go where it was supposed to go. "Let not the things of the earth hinder you," they said in their own words. "Let nothing that transpired while you lived hinder you. Let nothing trouble you now."

It is said that for close family and friends one year is the time for mourning, a time to show respect and restraint in our actions. But if this cannot be done, then ten days is the time to mourn. They also tell us that the death of a beloved person helps us all to become better aware of our own mortality, of the ways we choose to live and the paths we choose to walk. In a short time, we ourselves will be in that place, preparing to take that journey.

At the end of the day, everyone joined in a feast. Before anyone could partake in it, a special plate was prepared with every kind of food and was set aside. Either a person of the same sex and age who was close to the one who has died was to eat this meal, or it would be used as an offering to the spirit. On this night it was agreed that her husband would offer the special dish to the spirit.

He carried the spirit plate into the woods and left it alongside an old oak. On his way back, he stopped and gazed up at the stars, and he could sense the spirit of his wife all around him. Death had freed her from the pain of a body wrought with cancer. Now she was spirit, free in the Mystery, and he felt her everywhere. It was as if she was in the air he breathed. And she began to fill up the deep sense of emptiness he felt. He suddenly became aware of the newness of what was now. In a way it consoled him; in a way it frightened him.

In the moments that followed, his grief once again overcame him, and he wept from a place deep within his being. He remembered that the elders had encouraged him to cry. "Your tears carry the emotions of your grief and run in sacred streams," they said, "but they can become like poison to the body if they are withheld." He was told that by allowing himself to grieve in this way, he would also be honoring his feelings and the process that his mind and heart would need to heal.

As he struggled with his sorrow, he found a hint of comfort in knowing that, even if he lived to be an old man, someday, in some way, he would join her in the Mystery once again.

He reached into his pocket and pulled out a knife he had taken from the feast. His tears fell to the ground, and so did a significant clump of his long hair. Now people could see, whether they knew him or not, that he was a man in grief. And though in time it would grow back new and long, now he had cut off a part of his identity, for part of his identity belonged to her.

In the distance, he could hear the quiet voices of relatives and friends, and he suddenly felt an overwhelming sense of gratitude for those in their families and those friends who came to help, and or those who would be there when the ceremonies were done and through the dark days of grieving that would follow.

During that mourning time, he gave away his wife's things to those who helped her in life and death. At the end of the cycle of the four seasons, one year to the day she died, another ceremony would take place. It would honor her memory, and her husband and children would be told that death and gloom no longer surrounded them.

They would recall the ancient prayer: Now may the light of the sun shine into your hearts, and may you know happiness once again.

And those taking part in this ceremony would also express gratitude to the spirit of this Mother of the People for continuing its journey into the Mystery, and they would encourage the spirit to make the final jump to the other side:

> Let not the things of the earth
> that delighted you cause you to linger.
> Do not allow the things of the earth
> that troubled you to hinder you now.
> Now we release you, for it is true
> that it is no longer possible for us
> to walk about together on the earth.

In Beauty's Way, it is done.

PART V

DREAMS AND VISIONS

*The most beautiful experience we can have
is the mysterious.
It is the fundamental emotion that stands
at the cradle of true art and true science.
Whoever does not know it is as good as dead,
and his eyes are dimmed.*

— Albert Einstein

27

THE RITUAL OF THE DREAM CATCHER

Cradle Song
(Creek)

Down the stream
You hear the noise of her going
That is what they say
Up the stream
Running unseen
Running unseen
Up the stream
You hear the noise of her going
That is what they say
Running unseen
Running unseen

W hat was it like when Anibikaashi, Spider Woman, lived among the Original People? At best, we can only close our eyes and imagine.

Did she inhabit the spirit realm, and make herself available to the Anishinaabeg only through their dreams? Or did she dwell in their physical reality as well? Though it may stretch our imaginations to think of this wondrous being living among the people of so long ago, one thing we know is certain: the memory of Anibikaashi remains not solely as a myth timelessly embellished in the old stories, but as a living presence in the racial memory of the People, expressed through their dreams and their art.

She may have returned to her home in the other realm of dreamtime, or she may have departed for another home among the stars, but her image still manifests itself in the spider relatives that live among us today and in the spirit beings who appear in our dreams.

For this reason, we always show respect for spiders. If they come to inhabit a place that may intrude on us, we ask their permission, and then perhaps remove them to another location. In this way we acknowledge the goodness of Anibikaashi, and our respect for her memory. For now we can only see her dimly in their image, and through the mists of that memory in our dreamtime that still connects us to her and to the wonderful gift she left behind.

For as long as could be remembered, as far back as when the Anishinaabeg lived along the shores and mountains of the northeast coast, Spider Woman had cared for the People. But then her children grew restless and, for whatever reasons humans have to leave what they have always known, they began their migration west, following the journey of their tribal destiny.

Anibikaashi, who had cared for them since their creation, grew concerned, for she would not be able to protect them once they dispersed across the land.

It has been told by the elders of many generations that we humans were dreamed into existence by the Great Mystery, and that even the

Earth was dreamed into being. We have been taught that all forms of life that must sleep have dreams, and dreams can have great power.

And so, Spider Woman, seeking to protect her children, went to sleep and had a dream. In this dream a spirit came to her and showed her how to help ensure the safety of all her children, and all her children's children for as long as the People lived.

When Spider Woman awoke, she began teaching the grandmothers, aunts, sisters, and mothers how to make magical webs for the newborn babies of each generation.

She taught them how to make a hoop of willow, and to weave sinew or nettle-stalk cord into a web-like design, like the webs she makes. She showed them how to leave a small opening, a tiny hole, in the center of the web. Some say that she also instructed them to place something shiny in the web, though others believe that this idea may have come to the People in their own dreams later on.

Still, it is widely believed today that the glitter of a shiny object attracts mischievous or harmful entities toward it, and that the web itself catches any malevolent spirits, feelings, or thoughts that could be disturbing to the babies. Spider Woman said that only good thoughts and feelings would be able to pass through the center of the web and enter their dreamtime.

It is believed among the first People that the harmful and disturbing thoughts and spirits captured in the web during the night dissipate, like morning dewdrops on the grass, in the first rays of light from Father Sun.

And so the People designed their webs just as Spider Woman had instructed, and since that time long ago when the Anishinaabeg dispersed and migrated west, dream catchers have been used to help protect the babies.

Today, Native People all over the Americas make magical dream catchers, for now they are used to protect the dreamtime of children everywhere.

And everywhere, where spiders weave webs and dream catchers hang in windows and over children's beds, humans will sleep and dream.

Dream Song of a Woman
(Papago)

On top of the mountain,
I do not myself know where.
I wandered where my mind and my heart
seemed to be lost.
I wandered away.

28

A CEREMONY FOR THE DREAM

Among the First People who lived along the southern shores of Turtle Island were those who tell of a time when the trees were created.

It is said that the first tree to receive the breath of life, the breath of the Great Mystery, was the cedar. And that is why it smells so sweet. They say the sweet scent of the cedar induces dreaming.

It is said that another world exists besides this one — the dream world where the Mystery speaks through the spirits of other beings.

And it is also said that this is how we can travel to the far reaches of the universe, or even into different dimensions of time and space beyond our physical realities and limitations.

The whole past week had been stressful. She had been working on herself, trying to get a grip on her life, trying to remember her interior child, and trying to reconnect with her dreamtime once again.

For she has not been doing much dreaming lately, maybe because she is overtired. She wants to dream again.

Let me burn some cedar, she says. Not much, just enough to smoke my room, and help me dream.

She places the green tips and red stick shavings of cedar in an ocean shell about the size of her hand, and slowly lights it. She holds the source of the fragrant, sacred smoke and stands by her bed. Slowly, in the contemplative motion of a prayer, she moves the shell sunwise in a circle in front of her.

She does this four times, and closes her eyes. The sweet scent of the cedar stirs cellular memories, and pleasant feelings trickle down from her mind through her heart and into her soul.

When she is done, she places the shell on her night stand and watches the last embers fade in the swirling smoke. She turns off the light and slips into bed contented and secure. And, with a slight sense of anticipation, a wisp of hope, she shuts her eyes and drifts toward sleep.

Now if you were a spirit of goodness, and you could see her sleep that night, you would know that she was traveling in dreamtime, and you could smell the sweet scent of cedar mingling with the stars.

29

THE TURTLE DREAM: I AM THE MAKER

For Grandmother Sara Smith of Six Nations

It is deep within the sacred place inside our own hearts that we journey through the dark waters of the dream world as spirit, traveling alone across the invisible spaces to other worlds where the Ancestors come to share their love and their teachings with us, so that we may see things as they truly are. . . .

BY DENNIS HARRISON

I t was in this holy dreamtime that a young man slept in his little house by the sea. The moon was nearly full and the night was filled with stars. The sweet song of Mother Ocean's waves upon the shore and her gentle breath through the palms helped his spirit to float peacefully beyond, past the dark, silent waters of the void where he heard Great Grandmother speak to him.

I am the Maker. And I am the faith in Abundance.

In the darkness of the dreamworld he could not yet see, but her presence and the sound of her voice pounded in his chest like the thunder of a great medicine drum. He stood silently in the blackness of the void, his heart racing and his eyes straining to see when, like a gentle dawn, a red golden glow of light slowly rose from the shadows and the one who had spoken became visible to him.

He stood in awe, his eyes wide with amazement, for the Great Grandmother had come to him in the form of a giant sea turtle! She was greater in size and more beautiful than anything he had ever seen. The back of her shell rose up like a blue-green mountain into the night sky. Her huge head, wide as three of his arm lengths, bent forward, as if in prayer.

He could see her clearly now, for her entire being radiated the sacred glow that encircled them both in a sacred hoop of golden light.

The ancient lines and wrinkles of her face held untold stories of the Mystery, and her dark, watery eyes gazed lovingly upon him with a beauty and compassion he had never known. He stood before her in the sand, beside the great ocean from which she had come to make her nest.

Without speaking, the young man thought: The Mystery reveals itself to me as a giant sea turtle . . . a symbol of creation!

Hearing his thoughts, Great Grandmother slowly turned her head and looked deep into his eyes and asked:

Who is the Maker if not I?

The young man's eyes filled with tears, for his heart now knew the profound truth of her words. In that moment, Great Grandmother had given him wisdom: She was the Maker of All Things, and every woman who brings forth life, be she turtle, dolphin, wolf, spider, or human, is the Maker, and should be so respected and honored.

Great tears began to flow from the dark pools of Grandmother's eyes. Her voice was weary, but loving and gentle.

You must have faith. You must believe that if you share there is always bounty . . . that there is always goodness . . . and that always, there is enough love.

With a nod, Grandmother bowed her head and smiled at him.

There is never any need to fear. You and your brother are children of the Mystery, and you are both so loved. All that you need is given to you with such love.

With these words, Grandmother Turtle swept away the sand beneath her and nestled her great being close to the earth. Her breath became heavy, and she strained as she turned to him.

Now is the time for you to bring forth all the beauty and all the love that is within you, just as I now bring forth all the wonder that is within me.

With a great sigh, Grandmother Turtle closed her eyes and began to release her eggs gently into the sand. Each egg was a giant white orb that radiated the same red-golden glow as the Maker herself. One after another they came from her like small planets or stars in an endless flow of creation.

As he gazed upon the Holy vision before him, the young man understood in his heart the reason for Her flow of tears. Exhausted from her work, she slowly lifted her head so she could again look deep into his eyes.

I know that so many of my children will not live. They will not sur-vive the storms and the currents and all those who would do them harm. But still, I bring them forth, all of them, with such hope and faith, for each one carries the promise of goodness and hope.

It was his tears that told Great Grandmother that he understood her message with his heart, and she nodded and smiled sweetly.

You who are my children have the goodness and the courage to endure all things . . . to hope all things . . . to dream all things . . . and to become all things . . . for yourselves, and for all the children who will follow you.

The young man moved closer and sat quietly with her, in the Sacred Place she had created.

After a time, a soft veil of darkness fell over the young man's eyes, and he felt himself gently begin to return from the dreamworld. When he awoke, his eyes were still wet with tears, but his heart was filled with love and thankfulness for this dream. The holiness of it was still all around him, and filled his tiny room and beyond.

Slowly he arose from his bed and walked out into the moonlight with his pipe and pouch of sacred tobacco to offer prayers of gratitude for the sacred journey he had been given.

He looked up into the night sky and could not believe his eyes! The moon was shining with the same red-golden glow that Grandmother Turtle had created in his dream! His laughter and cries of joy and thankfulness filled the air, and soon awoke his brother, who came running.

The two brothers sat together beneath the stars, and upon the pipe the young man told his brother of his journey through dreamtime and the teaching that had been given to them both.

Suddenly, there in the golden glow of Grandmother Moon, they saw them: baby turtles, hundreds of them, coming up out of the sand from their nest, from Her, one after another, in an endless flow of hope and love.

30

A MAN SEEKS HIS PURPOSE IN THE MYSTERY

And while I stood there
I saw more than I can tell, and
I understood more than I saw:
for I was seeing in a sacred manner
the shapes of things in the spirit,
and the shape of all shapes as they must
live together like one being.

— Black Elk, *Black Elk Speaks*

There was once a time when the ritual of seeking a vision was as important and as much a part of a man's life as his birth and death.

It has been said that women are born with an innate understanding, an awareness of their primary purpose of procreation and co-creation. Though some women choose not to fulfill their purpose of procreation, they still have the power of creation, and find other ways to become fulfilled.

It has been said that the reason why it seems that more men than women are so often compelled to create things — paintings, buildings, books, poems, sculptures — is because men are not born with that power of creation. This is not to say women cannot do any of these things, for they can. Art forms and other creations by women are among the most beautiful in the world. But only women possess the sacred power of procreation, and men, it is said, are more driven to try and experience it through other forms.

It has been said that because men are not able to create life, they tend to be drawn more toward death. For one aspect of the nature of their power has always been and remains one that is destructive. Man can be a killer, a destroyer of life.

For this reason, more than likely, women did not beat upon the warrior's drum. Though there were women warriors, they were the exception, born out of necessity. On the warrior's drum were sung songs of death; a woman was regarded as the giver of life. Those powers would hurt each other if they came into contact.

It has been said too that men are the ones who often clear the fields before planting, because the power of man is one of destroyer and taker of life. Once the fields are cleared and seeds are placed in the earth, it is often the women who care for the gardens and nurture the life of growing things, though men do these things too.

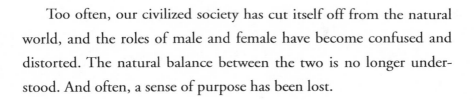

Too often, our civilized society has cut itself off from the natural world, and the roles of male and female have become confused and distorted. The natural balance between the two is no longer understood. And often, a sense of purpose has been lost.

If a man in civilized society is not properly guided, and cannot find the space, the place, for his creative energies, those energies can become twisted and destructive. Men can become overwhelmed by their destructive energies, or they can deny them completely. Either way, they have forgotten, or never knew, how to respect and honor their own powers of creation, in all their aspects.

And without a sense of purpose, men often try to fill their emptiness with possessions, attempting to fool themselves into thinking that real power is connected to consumption and wealth.

These men often have no connection, conscious or otherwise, to the sacredness of life, and they can become forces of destruction on the body of Mother Earth. The old ones say that such men are without vision, that these men lack the spirit that transcends the world and connects them to the sacred and mysterious. And so they destroy what is beautiful. They have no sense of their place in the great Circle of Life. And so they mutate, like cells gone awry, and they turn into killers, consuming everything beneficial until, like now, they threaten the very survival of their species and of the earth as we know her.

That is why it was believed a man must seek an understanding of his place in this world and in this universe. He must discover the ways and paths of power he can walk that can contribute to the welfare of the earth and the perpetuation of the Circle of Life.

It seems that all other life forms have a sense of purpose within the Circle. Even the smallest creatures know their individual purpose. An ant knows — not with his head, but he knows. Only civilized men appear to have lost their purpose, or maybe they have not yet evolved to the degree where they are even aware of it.

It seems that man, civilized and primal, is born without this kind of innate knowing. Men have to seek their place. They have to find a sense of purpose in life, a purpose that enables them to direct the destructive and violent elements of their nature toward more creative and beneficial forms of expression. This is where the ritual for the vision quest begins.

In many primal cultures the young men, especially, would take part in this spiritual quest, but the age and time of life for a man to seek a vision varies, for it is the time when he recognizes that he lacks

purpose and meaning, and realizes that he is losing his conscious connection to the sacredness of the earth, and to the Mystery. If he doesn't
fulfill the need that quietly emanates from his heart, he will become a
man without a vision, and among the People it is said that a man without a vision cannot be trusted; he is only half a man.

Perhaps this is true because the vision comes right out of the Great
Mystery and speaks directly to the one seeking it. And since so much
of the ability to receive such a gift comes from a man's heart, a vision
granted in this way can only help a man serve the People honorably
and do good for the Earth.

The ritual itself varies from people to people and land to land.
Sometimes just by walking the path of heart and goodwill, through
the struggle involved in that walk, a man can be accessible to the
vision. Or maybe he has a specialness about him that allows the vision
to unfold even when he is still a boy. Such experiences have occurred
at times to men.

But usually, at some point in his quest, a man seeking a vision
cuts himself off from other people and from man-made things, and
he does not eat or drink. Instead, he calls on that power that is
within him, the power that is within all things, and in the silence he

contemplates his place in the universe, and his feelings for life grow deeper, until they reach the depths of his being, the essence of his soul.

He may be drawn up with his knees pressed together, sitting quietly in the crotch of a great cedar, aware of the sounds around him, aware of how the sky people are mirrored in the lake he looks upon.

He may be crouched down in a tiny pit, praying on the top of a mountain, while the wings of a great bird hit his back and head as it circles around him.

He may walk the songlines of the ancestors in his dreamtime.

And then, "from his own juices," as it is said, a vision may come, perhaps at that moment, perhaps not. Perhaps at some time in the future when he least expects it, a time when his heart is open and his spirit becomes aware of itself, the Great Mystery will speak to him in a way that is unique, powerful, unimaginable, and truly sacred.

31

CRYING FOR A VISION

Carrying My Mind Around
(Tlingit)

My own mind is very hard on me.
It is just as if I were carrying my mind around.
What is the matter with you?

The glistening waters of the gulf look so refreshing, but he cannot drink from them, and his lips remain swollen and dry. Only the moisture from the soft offshore breeze gives him some relief.

Water. He has not had any for three days, nor has he had anything to eat. It is part of the ritual of the old ways, this quest for some greater insight, for some deeper understanding of his place in the Mystery, some sign that will enable him to continue.

In his mind's eye he imagines water running in streams, laughing over rocks made smooth by time; water, cool and clear, pure and life-giving. It took these two days to reconnect his consciousness to those elements of life without which he knew he could not exist.

Water, Earth, Air, Wind, and Fire....

What does it take for a man who has lived more than half a century to come to that place where he sits, naked and alone, under a burning summer sun, removed from human contact, weakened and weeping? Why would anyone choose to deprive his body in this way? What pain does his heart know? What burden weighs so heavily that he feels as if he were carrying his mind around?

This is not the first time he has attempted such a ritual. This is not the first time he became aware of his need to seek a vision in the old way. For it is a need that runs so deep that it reaches down into his primal essence, into that very first seed of Original Instruction.

When he was younger and trying to make his way in the world, he seemed to almost all at once begin losing everything he had held dear to him and everyone he had held close. Even the innocence he had retained in his young life was stolen away.

Lies, deceit, betrayal, disease, greed. These were some of the

shadow spirits stalking the world, dark aspects of the human condition that dogged his bright youthful intentions until they nearly
extinguished the light of his spirit, and he collapsed into the strong
arms of his old uncle.

It was at this point, as it is supposed to be, when the generation
closest to the Mystery reaches out to the ones still struggling to find
their way. His old uncle took from the past a tradition that would
help his young nephew to find the balance in his life and to know that
if he was to continue to walk a path of heart then it was time — time
for him to seek a vision in the old way. It was time to find a sacred
place, a place to meditate and pray, a place away from man-made
structures of concrete and steel, removed from the industrial noises of
cars and machines. It was time to find a place closer to the natural
world of living, growing things, connected to the wind's whisper over
water and to the rush of waves breaking on the shore.

Under the guidance of his uncle, the young man took a small
medicine stone and his eagle feather and went to a deserted beach
near the place where he had been raised. And there, where time itself
is like the sea, with no beginning and no end, at once now and forever, there among the drifting dunes and tall golden sea oats, he drew
a circle in the bone-white sand and remained within its circumference,

contemplating with his intercessors of stone and feather the purpose of his being.

Years later, he is no longer young, and no longer just discovering the shadow side of the world. He has become the elder, a man filled with a lifetime of experience, yet he once again finds himself crying for all that he has loved and all that he has lost, crying for those moments when death came to those he loved, his uncle, his wife, so many others, always too soon it seemed and too often unexpected. And he cries for the blessings of love that he was able to know, the gifts that love provided along the way.

And so, in the late autumn of this life cycle, approaching the fourth and final hill of his journey, he breathes in the salty, moist air on this third day and cries out into this Great Holy Mystery that has provided him this life.

He cries for the Earth and the animals. His breath bursts from that place deep inside of him, and expresses in sound without words his deep sense of sorrow for life denied and deprived, for a Mother dying in ways that he has come to know.

He cries for the dolphins and whales, for the plants and trees, and for the swirling feathered clouds of gulls and swooping pelicans he sees now, circling and diving through the air he breathes.

He cries for all the great and small life forms of the world, and for all those who have suffered too much under the crushing waves of human civilization.

He needs to know now that the meaning and purpose of his life has not been destroyed by civilized men. He needs to know that his ability to love has not been lost in the debris of their thinking, their waste, and contamination.

And so he cries for a vision in the old way, for something that will help him find the balance again, so that he may help those who are in need.

Water, Earth, Air, Wind, and Fire....

A soft breeze brushes the plumes on the eagle feather he has placed on the ground. He crouches close to the body of the Earth and leans toward the feather. He picks it up and twirls it in his fingers. A sudden gust sweeps across the water of the gulf onto the beach and across his face. It is a caress out of the Mystery itself, and he calls out his gratitude, for the joy he has known and for all those he has loved.

He feels them with him at this moment on the beach. He senses in the vibrations of his voice the pain that comes from his struggle; it feels that the sweeping motion of the feather in his hand casts his words into the wind. It feels that it has been through his struggle that he has been allowed to experience the balance of it all.

His bitterness dissipates in streams of sweat, that hard bitterness he had acquired over time from his encounters with all those shadow people who lack that special spirit-knowing, who have no inner awareness of their own lives and of their own sense of purpose in the Mystery. They are the shadow people who proclaim the right to defile the sacred and exploit the beautiful.

In the heat of the summer sun, influenced by the forces of nature around him and within him, his body has begun its purification. And the heat that had saturated his skin now cools in the wind.

Water, Earth, Air, Wind, and Fire....

The early light of the fourth day's dawn slowly turns the blue velvet sky bright, and he watches the water with blurry eyes as the sun rises and transcends into the dancing light of a million suns, into galaxies spiraling through his mind, into the pulsing radiance of quasars and the white tails of shooting stars. His mind expands with the universe. How truly incomprehensible it all is. His own sense of self is so small at this moment that the grueling weight of his despair and anguish seems insignificant, and it lifts, evaporating in the mist, with no more weight to overpower him.

The glitter of those million suns quietly illuminates all those places in his heart where the dark spirits of the human condition had over the years cast long shadows. And now, the awareness of a universe teeming with life and energy makes his own life, with all its hard and painful experiences, feel much less important after all. And yet it is this very thought that enables him to once again become conscious and aware that he is still a vital part of this infinite Totality that always was and will always be. . . .

And the million suns suspended in thought become living memories, warming that part of his heart made cold by their absence.

At this moment past, present, and future intertwine like a spider's web, and everything is woven into Oneness, and he no longer feels so isolated and alone, uncertain of his place and his worth. He no longer feels pulled further into the depths of depression by human meanness, power, and greed. He no longer acquiesces to the dark, cold spaces between all those stars of memory. He feels the great balance of all creation, built on bursts of light.

He feels connected to the spirits of a million suns, and the warmth of this awareness softens the heart hardened over time, and the quiet beauty of their starlight brightens the dense, dark places in the mind he has carried around.

The starlight of those million suns guides him now out of that darkness into the last phase of his life and into the vision he has cried to receive, lifting his spirit higher and higher. . . .

Water, Earth, Air, Wind, and Fire.

Prayer to the Sun

(Teton)

Okohe! okohe! natosi! ito!

Sun, take pity on me; take pity on me.
Old age, old age,
I am praying to your old age,
For that I have chosen.
Your children, morning star,
 seven stars,
the bunched stars, these and all stars,
We can call on them for help.
I have called on them.
Take pity on me;
Take pity that I may lead a good life.
That which is above, now I choose.
Take pity on me.

Iyo!
Take pity on me; take pity on me;
 take heed.

PART VI

SEASONS AND HEALING

A human being is part of the whole,
called by us the 'universe,'
limited in time and space....
Our task must be to free ourselves from our prison
by widening our circle of compassion
to embrace all humanity and the whole of nature
in its beauty.

— Albert Einstein

CHANGE: FEARED AND CELEBRATED

I, Nezahualcoatl, ask this:
Is it true one really lives on the earth?
Not forever on the earth,
only a little while here.
Though it be jade it falls apart,
though it be gold it wears away,
though it be quetzal plumage it is torn asunder.
Not forever on the earth,
only a little while here. . . .

— from the poet King Nezahualcoatl,
the wise and famous lord of Tezcoco (1402–1472)

If there is one certainty in the universe that we are indeed aware of, if there is one notion that rings true compared to all that we think we know, if there is one aspect of this Great Holy Mystery that we both fear and celebrate, if there is one thing that we resist and embrace, it is change.

Without change could any species develop the physical characteristics necessary for survival? Without change could our consciousness of our relationship to all things help us to evolve and peacefully coexist? Without change would we learn to appreciate and honor each experience, each moment, and each other?

In a sacred place called Stonehenge, among the rolling hills of England, the placement of great stones brought from miles away, stones weighing tons, stones cut and positioned in a great circle, measure and mark the perpetual motion of change by the ever-moving position of the sun in the sky.

The ancient Celts in Northern Ireland built mounds of earth to connect themselves more closely to the solar and lunar events that mark the passage of seasons and the earth's relationship to other celestial bodies.

On Easter Island, the faces carved long ago in stone gaze out toward the sea and up to the sky, and their expressions seem to exhibit an awareness that we are indeed connected to other worlds and other times. These faces of beings known only perhaps through our primal memories appear to cry out to us that change will come; inevitably, change must come to everything.

In Central America, the ancient Mayans achieved a way of living and of creating human expression that is perhaps unsurpassed artistically in our known human history. These people have left behind one of the greatest designs on earth that acknowledges and celebrates the one universal constant on which we can all depend — change.

In the Yucatàn peninsula of Mexico, at a place called Chichén Itza, the Mayans built a tall pyramid now called El Castillo (The Castle). On each of its four sides it has a staircase of more than a hundred steps leading to the top. At the bottom of the pyramid are large snake heads, and the bodies of the snakes are made from triangular stones that go up each side of the staircases. On the day of the summer solstice, when the sun is at its exact highest point in the sky, the stone snake bodies appear to move down the staircases. At no other time do they appear to move.

The Mayan people also created a calendar, as accurate as any modern science has developed, that served as a model for the one we have today, which records each day of our solar year and marks each phase of our thirteen full moons. The Mayans also recorded cosmic cycles, many lost to civilized man because he burned them out of fear.

Among many of the first nations of North America, our continent is called Turtle Island, for ancient stories embellished the idea that the first land here was originally supported on the back of a great turtle. Among many of the indigenous peoples of North America, creation accounts of various nations record similar versions of the story of a female being who came from the Sky World or Star Nation and landed upon the earth that had formed on the back of the turtle. The accounts often describe her giving birth to a daughter of this Earth, who became pregnant with twin brothers who had supernatural abilities and helped form the North American continent.

In a way that helped them symbolically reconnect with this primal past, the turtle shell became a calendar of sorts, used to record the times when certain ceremonies were held to honor the gifts of planting and harvest, and to acknowledge Grandmother Moon's changing influences on Mother Earth and other events that mark the passage of time.

It has been said that on the back of each turtle shell are thirteen squares, one for each moon in a complete earth year.

Among the great orators of human history stands Sealth, a Suquamish-Duwamish leader also known as Chief Seattle. In one of the most poignant and flawless examples of the oral tradition, this man of wisdom and eloquence recognized the power and inevitability of change when he acknowledged the vanquishing of Native Americans from their own country, and he said that no race of people on this earth is excluded from this one universal absolute:

> *Tribe follows tribe, and nation follows nation,*
> *like the waves of the sea.*
> *It is the order of nature. . . .*

From stones cut and carved, from pyramids and calendars, through turtle shells and prophetic words, our ancient relatives still speak to us today, and tell us that change on this earth and in the universe is the one constant on which we can truly depend. It is the one aspect of everything we believe we know that remains unquestionably real — and if we are to dwell together in harmony and peace for the brief time that we are here, change must be acknowledged and honored.

Change is at the heart, at the root, of all our ceremonies. For in one way or another, whether we're acknowledging thanksgiving or in need of healing, our rituals are all about change.

Over a thousand years ago, in New Mexico's Chaco Canyon,

people called the Anasazi built Pueblo Bonito, the world's first giant apartment building. It stands five stories tall and contains more than eight hundred rooms, covering over three acres. It wasn't until the late 1800s that anything larger was built on the continent.

There were over a dozen other buildings like it in the area. But the grandeur of Pueblo Bonito was not merely in its size, it was in its nearly perfect environment. It was built in the form of a great circle, carefully designed and located so that the people lived in a relatively comfortable climate, warm in the winter, cool in the summer.

And Pueblo Bonito, and other similar constructions of the Anasazi, also marked the beginning of the seasons and phases of the moon, and each dwelling had kivas — small, circular, enclosed rooms — for meditation and prayer and ceremony.

Certainly from these age-old meditations and prayers came age-old questions and insights about the nature of time and its constant companion, change. Perhaps these questions were asked and answered in a way very much like that of poet-king Nezahualcoatl centuries ago:

Is it true one really lives on the earth?
Not forever on the earth, only a little while here. . . .

33

WINTER SOLSTICE CEREMONY

The Song of the Stars

We are the stars that sing,
We sing with our light.
We are the birds of fire,
We fly over the sky.
We make a road for spirits,
For the spirits to pass over....

When he was a boy he watched his grandfathers and elder uncles and other male relatives stand beneath the cold sky and welcome with the pipe and tobacco the coming of winter.

He watched as they directed their words of Thanksgiving toward the low slanting sun, even as the bitter cold bit down into their bones. He could smell the aroma of hominy soup wafting in the wintry air from the old woodstove, and hear the sounds of quiet voices coming from his grandmothers, aunts, and other female relations.

The elders told him, when he was a boy, that winter is a time when the earth must rest from her life-giving and nurturing; she needed this time to preserve strength for her own journey.

"Imagine," they said. "Imagine that the snow you see on the land is a blanket gifted from the Sky to cover his mate, the Earth, while she sleeps."

It is also a time, they said, "when Mother Earth needs to dream herself and reconnect in spirit ways to the Mystery of Life."

Gitchie Manitou Geezis, the Great Mystery Moon, waxes and wanes in the midst of winter's presence. "This is the time to become quiet," they told the boy, "and reflect on those things and people who are closest to you, and remember and acknowledge all they have given you. For the cold winds and the spirit of the cold winds will come and take their toll on those who are sick and those who have been weakened...."

They told him to be more aware of those he loves now, for this was a time for human beings to bond more closely together, to become aware that our own time here on earth remains cyclical and ephemeral.

"Winter is a time to think about our own Great Change," the old ones told the boy. "It will come, in its own time, sooner than we want. It's a time to reflect on our goodness, and to direct our prayers in ceremony at this time of power in the sacred presence of winter."

The boy was taught to honor the time of the solstice, when the path of the sun is lowest in the sky, farthest to the south, and when the days are short, and the stars seem so many and appear so close it is as though we can reach up and touch them. Then, the old ways teach us, we are to acknowledge the power of winter, and honor the journey of Mother Earth back toward the Sun Father. Like our ancestors did long ago, we must encourage her on that journey so that we may live. For if the voice of even one person can still be heard in this way, the old ones say that the earth will know she is loved by the people who are her children, and can continue her journey.

When he first joined his elders for the solstice ceremonies, the boy was told that, in all its cold power, winter is a time when life, and the spirit that animates it, can be made stronger. "It is a time to purify. A time to seek dreams that help guide and teach us. A time to reflect on where we came from, and who we are. A time to reflect on our relationship to All That Is."

They said that, during this season more than any other in the year, peace seemed to prevail everywhere. And so the old ones called these days Peacetime — the span of days between winter solstice and the new year. "It is a time of giving," they told him. "It is a time to invite Nokomo, the Spirit of Giving, into your home."

Then comes the dawn of one winter's solstice when he begins another Peacetime no longer as a boy, but as a man in the autumn of his life. The elders have all moved on, and guide him now only as misty spirits and distant memories.

He faces the low slanting sun and witnesses the new beginning of another winter. He stands looking north, in the direction of its origin, and speaks words of Thanksgiving, expressing his gratitude to the earth, the sky, the sun, the sea, the forests, and the fresh waters that flow beneath their icy surface.

Thank you for the beauty
I have known in this life.
And thank you even for the cold of my sorrow,
for it has enabled me to know the warmth of my joy
and to know there must be balance,
to see that without sorrow there would be no joy,
just as without darkness there would be no light.

Thank you for all you have provided me,
and for all the challenges and struggles
that I have encountered on this journey,
and for the ones that lie ahead.
I know that they are like your power,
for they keep my heart and spirit strong.

Now the elder who was a boy such a brief moment before acknowledges his gratitude for peace and once again invites Nokomo, the Spirit of Giving, into his home and into his life.

He looks down and stares at his reflection in the frozen mirror of time. His hair has turned white, like the snow, and he feels himself being drawn more closely now to the Earth and to the Mystery. He remembers the older people, with their step slowed, some with their bodies slightly bent with age, as they move toward her. For the Circle of Life, he has known all along, must always complete itself.

And now, one more time, he faces the cold Sun on this particular winter solstice, during this special Peacetime, more grateful than ever that he has been granted a life that has carried through to this last phase of the life cycle, the concluding part of this earth journey, heading for the Fourth Hill and, finally, for the stars.

34

SPRING EQUINOX CEREMONY

For the Earth, and for all of the life forms upon her, the powers of spring are birth and rebirth. It is the time of year of Creation, the time known as The Beginning of Newness.

As humans we have been given the gift of two legs to stand on, and of voices that can express and appreciate the sacred blessing of life itself. We can look back on the winter and recall fondly the memories of those we loved who have made their Great Change into the Mystery but leave our hearts filled with love and goodness.

The power of spring manifests, greater than any other time, the incredible gift of the sun, the gift of life. When the sun rises on the day of the spring equinox, we show our gratitude for the abundance that has been available to us in the Mystery, and we are thankful that all we need has been provided for us.

We release our fears of being without, knowing it is this fear of scarcity that can prevent All That Is from providing what we and our loved ones need to be healthy and honorable people through all the ever-changing cycles of life and time.

Spring is the time to acknowledge the power of growth, within us and throughout the world, to acknowledge not only the power within the seed that will spring forth with new life, but the power as well of those seeds that are ideas, for it is our thoughts that shape our world. We remember and cultivate the good thoughts that others have planted in us, and we remember that we plant our thoughts into others, as teachers and wise elders now, as we draw on life experiences and primal wisdom, and we must take care to pass on what we know is old and good.

Spring also reminds us that the power to abort lies within the mother. By observing nature we recognize that among all those seeds planted in Mother Earth, she will select only the ones she chooses to take root and bring forth new life, and she will abort the others. This great power belongs to her; it is a power she has never abused.

I stand in the color of the dawning spring sun,
facing the East.
I am in the presence of the Power
of Birth and Rebirth.

I thank the Great Mystery
for the Sun and Earth,
the wind and rain,
and for all those I have loved
who have made the Great Change.

I thank the Sun and the Earth
for their love and for their powers
to manifest the wondrous gift of life.

I thank the forces of Creation
for all the abundance that fills my life,
and pray that my fears of scarcity
will prove groundless, and dissolve.
May my loved ones have all they need
to be healthy and to live fully honorable lives.

May I remember the old teachings,
and the primal wisdom,
and may my thoughts, words, and actions
be beneficial and good.

May I complete the cycle of seasons
with a good heart,
filled with love and appreciation.
May I give my best to my people
and my world.

35

THE OLD WOMAN WHO WAS YOUNG: A CEREMONY FOR SPRING

For Sara of the Turtle Clan

The wise old woman of the Turtle Clan sat on the old rock along-side the old river, looking into the doe-brown eyes of her young relative sitting next to her. The girl who was becoming a woman had recently tried to end her short life of sixteen years.

"I am puzzled," the grandmother said. "Why would such a pretty and sweet young person want to end her earth walk so soon?"

She placed her hand on her granddaughter's knee. Her own life had seemed so short, she pondered. If only this young one could know how brief it all is...the flash of a firefly in the great scheme of things. She spoke again, careful not to impose judgment in her voice.

"You haven't completed your journey here," she said.

The grandmother looked in the direction of the tiny Indian violets opened in the crevices of the old stones. "They are the first to bloom in the spring, you know."

She paused again, appreciating their beauty, contemplating their will to live and their determination to celebrate life by showing themselves even as the last of the freezing rains would fall.

"A flower does not turn on itself."

The girl who was becoming a woman glanced up from her sneakers, first at the flowers, then at the source of this gentle, loving voice. Her attention did not focus on her grandmother's long silvery hair, the silky strands lifting slightly in the early spring breeze; she felt drawn more to the old eyes that still sparkled like a child's...eyes that were not dark like the deer's, as many of the girl's other relatives, but bright green, more like the moss of the old glistening rocks in the middle of the old river that moved past them in the warm noonday sun, or the kind of green that the budding willows wear during their rebirth this time of year, when everything seems to become new and alive again.

"I have no role model, Grandmother," the girl responded. "No one to look up to...no one to teach me...."

She etched a circle in the dark earth with the toe of her sneaker. It was not a conscious drawing, but the expression of a concept etched in her mind. "My mother drinks," she continued. Her voice quivered. One part of her felt angry, the other part just hurt. "My aunties drink.... My father I only see once in a while and when I do he's usually been drinkin'. And my brother was killed in that wreck last year ridin' home from college with his friends. The man who hit them was drunk."

The girl who had been sitting alongside the old woman sitting on the old rock suddenly stood, taking notice of a pair of cardinals that had just swooped down on a worm. "Look, Grandma!" she called. "The male stays so close to the female. It's like he watches out for her."

Then with a flick of a feather the birds returned to the nest. "Do you think they have babies?"

"Yes," the grandmother replied, "seems they have young ones to care for." She gazed up at the old elm as she spoke. Its new budding leaves enfolded the nest crafted in one of the tree's strong boughs. "It's like the spirit of new life is all around them," she said.

Then she leaned back, stretched, and took a deep breath. She thought, How good it feels to be alive.

"You know," she continued, "you mustn't think that only people can be your role models. Look around you. Your teachers are every-where. They're among the plants and the trees. They're among the animals and birds. They dwell in the earth among the insects. They live in the sea among the dolphins and whales. These are our relatives, and they've been our teachers always. Without them, how would people know how to live?"

The old woman of the Turtle Clan stood and walked to where the young woman who was still a girl was standing alone gazing up at the elm. "The way we need to live is in that tree . . . is in that nest . . . is everywhere our Mother Earth provides life that is older and wiser than we are. For many of us have forgotten how to live." She pointed up. "But they have not forgotten. You can learn so much by watching them. . . .

"They are your role models. They are your teachers."

They stood in silence together.

"Now come," said the old woman who seemed so young. She held out a deerskin pouch and offered it to her granddaughter. "Take a pinch of this special tobacco kept in this gift from our brother, the deer. Take some into your hand if you like."

The young woman who nearly took her own life but a short time ago reached in with her delicate fingers and took the tobacco.

"Now make your prayers of gratitude," the old woman encouraged, "for life. . . . Sprinkle them like seeds under this old elm in recognition of the spring and the Beginning of Newness."

As time and the cycles of life continued those seeds of prayer would grow, and the woman who was once young would one day return to this place by the old river, where the old elm still lived and the cardinals had made their nest. This became her ceremony. She would come back every spring equinox, every year for the rest of her long and wonderful life.

And she would bring her children and her grandchildren there to see those hardy Indian violets still blooming between the crevices of the old rocks with that same determination to celebrate life, and she would remember the old woman of the Turtle Clan who was always young in her old voice of wisdom and in her old green eyes of spring.

She would remember the animals and the birds. She would remember her teachers of the gift of life.

3 6

A HEALING SONG

Earth and Sky need time to heal.
Animals need time to heal.
Birds and Insects,
And Plants and Trees,
Each needs time to heal.
Dolphins need time to heal,
And Whales,
And Shellfish and Fish,
All need time to heal.

Men need time to heal,
Women need time to heal,
And our children need time to heal.

Now, in the healing time,
Now, in the healing time.

37

A CEREMONY OF HEALING

He was stretched out on his back, lying on an Indian blanket. His eyes were shut, and he was thinking about everything that had gone on to bring him to this point. Throughout it all, the pain in his side had worsened. His knees ached, and the surface of his skin around his knees and his side burned to the touch with the same kind of intensity as the fire that flickered from the flames of several candles placed around the room.

The smoke of sweetgrass and the sweet scent of cedar mingled in the air, enveloping him. An old woman sitting next to him said, "Relax . . . relax. Exhale the negative energy. Breathe in the good."

Moments before, they had sat facing each other across the blanket, and he had held a clay cup in his hands. "Do you like it?" she asked. "Do you like how it feels in your hands?"

He pressed his palms against the smooth glazed surface, and nodded.

She smiled. "I've a strong desire to do more work with the earth form, you know," she said.

He gripped the cup and examined it carefully, feeling the heat from the tea it contained.

"I love the malleability of clay," she said. "I love the organic smell, the feel of old, old earth and knowing it is the earth, smelling of decay, rich with potential." She too looked at the cup in his hands. "All one has to do," she said, "is become familiar with it, and be able to grasp it and feel your way through it into its form."

She smiled at her thought, at her words. "But even though it's so malleable, you have to notice what's there, what's inside it, and not impose your will on it, and not force an opinion, even an idea, upon it."

He pressed the clay cup to his lips once again and sipped the tea.

It tasted bittersweet, not unlike other things in his life. But why all this talk of clay?

"Because clay is so soft, and so transmutable," she said, responding as if she had heard the thought, sensing in the way that she did, "and it can become hard as stone."

His back stiffened, and he touched his side where the pain was. He closed his eyes, and then in some way the feelings that her words had conjured led him to travel somewhere far beyond his conscious mind, and to see deep into his heart. Somehow the emotions that emerged on the journey could be felt in the very cells of his physical existence. . . .

He blinked as if surfacing from a trance and was startled by his own bright reflection gazing up at him from within his cup of tea. He looked over again at the old woman, who sat peacefully still and silent, and felt the strange feeling that all their conversation had been imagined, projected in some way from their thoughts. It felt as if it had all taken place in his mind, and not a word had been spoken.

He slowly shook his head, trying to clear it and to ponder what had happened and what had been said. Then he sipped the special tea again, and recalled watching her prepare the tea, praying over the cup while she dropped in the roots, one by one.

This was the medicine root she had gathered at the end of last summer, she told him. When she was young, she had discovered the power of this root, and pledged to use its spirit wisely. And now the spirit of the plant would aid in his healing.

She told him while he watched her brewing it that to acknowledge the root is to express gratitude to the source of our own roots, that to acknowledge the root of anything was to recognize the origin of its manifestation.

And while he drank the tea, feeling its medicine journey into his being, she told him how important it was to live in the balance. She said that choosing the path of heart was essential for his spiritual as well as his physical being, and that choosing that path also presented many challenges. She said it was part of the balance.

"But stay true to your heart," she said, "no matter what befalls you or how hard you may fall from the path. Continue to listen to your heart and trust in the balance."

While she placed the end of the sweetgrass braid in the fire of the nearest candle, she told him she imagined everyone grows weary of the struggle, at some point in his life, in her life. Some even leave the path of heart and lose their way. She said we were allowed to get lost along the path of heart, but only seven times. "And finding the way back is not easy," she said. "And it only gets harder the longer one stays away."

A serpent of smoke formed from the burning braid and swirled away from the candle, coiling in the hazy air, flitting its tongue, and then it swirled inside his own senses, the sweet medicine smoke filling his mind.

Then she asked him to talk to her, to tell her about himself. She held an eagle feather in her lap, and with her old eyes shut, she listened as he spoke about his life, and she slightly twirled the beaded stem, rubbing the tiny cut-glass beads with her long spindly fingers in the way a nun might pray on a rosary.

Now, stretched out on his back, eyes closed, he knew that it had come to this, that his life was in danger, that it was threatened by an illness sustained at the most basic level of his existence.

She had positioned herself just above his head, and was brushing the eagle feather across his face while she chanted in the old language a prayer song, singing words he did not understand.

The song came to her in a dream a long time ago, she had told him, and she sang it only and always while she worked with her medicine.

And while she sang over him, she fanned him with the feather, sweeping away the energy that had harbored around the origin of his pain, sweeping away any spirits born out of the emotions that could cause him harm.

He opened his eyes, his vision blurred. The candle lights glowed intensely, their fires small orbs of luminescence. He couldn't see the old woman, because she remained behind him, sitting peacefully still, the eagle feather on her lap now, her long fingers holding its beaded stem.

"I am not going to tell you that I will heal you," she said. "I don't presume to have the power to do that, but if you're willing, and with your permission, I can serve as the conduit for the power of healing and perhaps that power will flow through my hands into you, and it will help heal you. It will work with the medicine of the root and help you heal."

There was a pause, then suddenly she was alongside of him, gazing into his eyes, silky strands of her white wispy hair shining in the silver light. "But that's only part of it," she said, and stood up straight and stretched. She was much taller than he first remembered. "The other part is within you."

She touched him, and he didn't see her hands but he felt them, feeling the fire that flowed out of them and into him, into his pain.

With his eyes shut he recalled seeing the image of his face in the cup of tea, and the soul that was revealed to him, and how the fire of her healing would burn deeper into the man he really was. And he could hear inside each cell the sorrow of what seemed like lifetimes being washed away by the sounds of a hard rain shaking from her turtle shell rattle. And he could feel his heart beating stronger while she beat on her deerskin drum. All the while, little spirit lights shot across the space of his mind, like energy sent from the stars.

Occasionally, she'd pause, and sometimes the silence would feel like a poignant moment from an old story, and then she would talk a bit, and show him where his emotions tended to "store up" inside him, and she would send a fire into that place with quiet, gentle force. She said that the fire that burned into him through her hands was the power, and that it was not hers.

He remembered not knowing if his eyes were open or closed, only that he saw a series of extraordinary images about himself that he couldn't retain. He remembered hearing the rattle, and how it made the soothing sound of cleansing rain sing within his mind. And he remembered seeing the tiny flickering fires of the candles and feeling the fire streaming from her hands.

Shadows danced round his blanket, and a new feeling, a new

awareness, danced like a joyful child inside his head. And all the while her words sang to him, as if out of a dream.

And then he awakened to another kind of consciousness, and she was bending over him, gesturing around him, spinning feelings of well-being with her long arms. Then she stopped, then she began to spin again.

"Man-made time is collapsing," she said, twirling her hands as if connecting something. "Pay attention to natural Time."

She said that it was hard for human beings today to live happily in unnatural time, that it was really impossible to be truly happy living that way. And as she brushed the tip of the eagle feather to her lips she said, "Even on the path of heart we can be drawn into the darkness of those who do not follow the path, even by those who have strayed from it and may be lost.

"Always try to stay connected to the beautiful," she said. "You must try to stay in the light of your true self."

It seemed as though Grandmother Spider had shifted Time within that small room, and he was traveling on this Indian blanket through a hole in the center of the web of life that she had re-created, and into a black celestial sea of Mystery where dewdrops of morning mist transcend into stars of great wisdom and brilliance, some of them telling about him, some of them telling about the whole world around him.

He gazed like an infant up through the sparkling web, and she said, again, how important it was for him, and for his family, and for his people, and for the world, that he remain on the path of heart.

"It means more than you think, more than you can ever know," she said.

She pointed through the smoky room and out the window. "Be more aware of the natural cycles of time," she said. "Watch the phases of the moon, and the movement of the sun's path across the sky. Watch the passing of the seasons. There is power in everything," she said, "and we are part of everything. And there is spirit in everything, and we are spirit too.

"Watch the animals and the birds. They live in natural Time. Pay attention to the trees and to the plants. Listen to your body and know that you are connected to the natural rhythms and cycles of Time and Mystery."

The tiny flames on the candles flickered near the sculptures of melted wax, and she shook her head slowly and said, "Try not to let the darkness of another take away your light. It is up to each of us whether we grow from our mistakes or not, for within our mistakes dwells either new wisdom, and new life, or atrophy — the atrophy of our potential, if we let our anger or our sorrow consume what is good in us, and what can still be good in us."

She brushed the top of the feather across the flame of the candle, nearly extinguishing it. "If we allow too much of our light to escape or to be absorbed in the shadow of another, we become weakened, and our spirit light dims."

Then she laughed, and made jokes about the nature of old age. Then she wept, and said there wasn't any time left to put off loving and taking care of Mother Earth. Then she was quiet, pondering something, and then she said it was getting harder for her to gather medicine, and she hoped someone would come along soon to learn these things from her.

All was quiet for a moment. Then he felt the energy to stand, on shaky legs at first.

They stood together on the porch in front of her house. She gestured gracefully with her long arms, pointing to the cloudless blue sky. "Can you see the stars?" she asked. Of course he couldn't, even as he strained to see beyond the sunlight. The old woman reflected momentarily on something and then headed back toward her front door. But just before she stepped inside, she paused one more time and turned back toward him.

"Stars during the daylight burn just as steadily, even if they aren't visible." She looked up with her old eyes. "The universe burns just as brightly without our knowledge or our witness."

Then she looked at him and smiled, and kept smiling as she slowly turned and went into her house and closed the door behind her.

As he watched her disappear, he could feel the child awaken within him again, and the world became like new again, and he felt himself dancing through the dream of his own healing and into a consciousness, an awareness, that he'd almost forgotten, dancing again on a hope and a prayer, dancing again on the path of heart.

RECOMMENDED READING

If you enjoyed *The Book of Ceremonies,* we highly recommend
these books from New World Library:

◉ *Neither Wolf Nor Dog: On Forgotten Roads with an Indian Elder* by
Kent Nerburn.

◉ *The Soul of an Indian: And Other Writings from Ohiyesa* edited by
Kent Nerburn.

◉ *The Wisdom of the Native Americans: Including the Soul of an Indian
and Other Writings from Ohiyesa and the Great Speeches of Red Jacket,
Chief Joseph, and Chief Seattle* edited by Kent Nerburn.

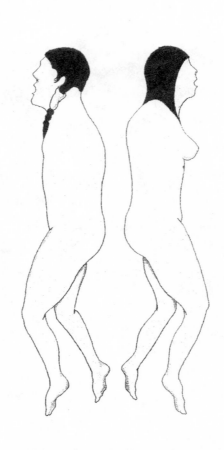

ABOUT THE AUTHOR

GABRIEL HORN (**White Deer of Autumn**) is a writer and associate professor who teaches writing, literature, and Native American philosophy. His other books include *Native Heart, Ceremony in the Circle of Life, The Great Change,* and *Contemplations of a Primal Mind.* He lives with his wife, Amy, in St. Petersburg, Florida.

CARISES HORN has been drawing ever since he could hold a pencil. By the time he was eleven years old his artistic renderings of dolphins decorated the walls and the quarterly news publications of the Dolphin Research Center in the Florida Keys. At ages thirteen and fourteen he won several artistic awards at Kituwah, an American Indian Education and Arts Exposition held in Asheville, North Carolina, and

his original thought forms appeared throughout the pages of his father's book *Contemplations of a Primal Mind*. A few years later he created the cover art for the book's second edition, published by the University Press of Florida. His work has also appeared in art galleries and been sold to private collections. He lives on the gulf coast of Florida.

N EW WORLD LIBRARY

is dedicated to publishing books and audio products
that inspire and challenge us
to improve the quality of our lives and our world.

Our products are available in bookstores everywhere.
For our catalog please contact:

New World Library
14 Pamaron Way
Novato, CA 94949

Telephone: (415) 884-2100 or (800) 972-6657
Fax: (415) 884-2199
Catalog requests: Ext. 50
Orders: Ext. 52

Email: escort@newworldlibrary.com
Website: www.newworldlibrary.com